Oliver Black is a professor of philosophy and law, and
has published widely in those fields. Until recently he
was also a City lawyer. His most recent novel, *The
Commune* (Ashgrove, 2014), is a comedy about old
people. He has published other fiction under a
pseudonym. He lives in London and Dorset with his
wife and cat.

SHRUNK

And Other Stories

Oliver Black

PROSPERO

First published in Great Britain in 2016 by Prospero Press.
www.prosperopress.net

A CIP catalogue record for this book is available from the British Library.

ISBN: 978-0-9928972-6-0

Set in Adobe Caslon Pro font

Book design and layout: Katharine Smith,
Heddon Publishing

Cover design: Laura Bamber

Contents

Shrunk

If you go to the doctor with a jumble of symptoms that baffle her, she is likely, once she has run out of tests to conduct and has got bored with you, to suggest that you see a psychotherapist, on the basis that, if you're not ill, you must be mad. That happened to me a couple of years ago. Symptoms, like children, are fascinating if they are your own, but boring if not, so I shall spare you the details of mine: in brief, they included fluish malaise, lassitude, faintness, dizziness and swollen glands, as well as some that are the therapist's bread and butter, such as feelings of anxiety, disorientation and unreality. Time to stop overworking, many friends said, and their diagnosis has never been bettered. Nevertheless Vera, my GP, claimed to think that there might be more to it – or did think that her colleagues would welcome a private patient – and therefore referred me to one Glenda Gibbon, whom she confidently predicted I would like very much.

My previous encounter with psychotherapy had been decades earlier, when delayed adolescence and its horrors hit me during my time as an undergraduate at Cambridge. The therapist, a young woman who pressed me to call her Osie, favoured folksy attire, and wooden clogs in particular. Her practice was at the old Addenbrooke's Hospital, which by then was almost disused, save for a maternity unit: distant wails of the newborn would occasionally reach me as I sat on a bench in the long and dismal Victorian corridor, inhaling the smell of Dettol and waiting for Osie, whose approach would be heralded by the Rossinian crescendo of an echoing clop-clop, as of a two-legged donkey. For our sessions we could have had any of the many deserted wards to ourselves, but we would meet in a large laundry-cupboard that still contained sheets and pillow-cases. On one occasion, when I was in full flow on the subject of my sexual fantasies, an oddly elderly nurse opened the door and squawked, having expected to find only the bedclothes. 'Where were we?' Osie lamely asked after the old dear had receded, but I couldn't pick up the threads.

Therapists are doubtless taught to conceal their emotions, but Osie seemed naturally wan. The only time a smile – a watery one – played on her lips was when I knocked one arm off my glasses while gesticulating. (Afterwards I managed to re-attach it with a matchstick and some dental floss: *nota bene*.) Intellectually she was no sprightlier: a student of formal logic, I was nettled by her fondness for erroneously accusing me of self-contradiction, and once she compounded the offence by remarking that what I had said was 'slightly' contradictory. Her mantra was the safe 'How do you feel about that?' – which she would utter even in response to my statements about my feelings.

The course was cut short by Osie's pregnancy, long concealed under her poncho. As I was soon to leave Cambridge, she put me in touch with a psychoanalyst in London. Her letter confirming the referral was sent, like one from the rodent officer, in a discreet brown envelope, but was addressed to me at my parents' house. Discretion was thus cast to the winds. My mother, assuming that a brown envelope bespoke a bill that she would be called on to pay, opened it in my absence and read 'Dear Oliver, you are right to continue treatment, especially for your sex problem.' We tacitly agreed not to discuss the matter, for my mother was one of those who would have preferred sex, let alone problematic sex, not to exist. 'When sex rears its ugly head' was one of her phrases.

The analyst, Herman Galberg, had more gravitas than Osie, and it seemed that no smile, watery or other, had played on his lips for decades, his face having the rigidity that can be induced by Parkinson's. So far as I could tell from his steady hand, that was not the cause in his case. At the end of our first session, I left my umbrella in his room and returned to collect it. 'I expect you can read volumes into that,' I quipped. In return he gazed at me like the Sphinx. Others have experienced the same sort of thing. My friend Moses, who exhausts his meagre salary on four-times-weekly analysis both for himself and, separately, his wife, frequents an analyst whose couch is covered by a woollen blanket with an open texture like that of Aertex shirts (*sanctae memoriae*). On one occasion Moses had a biro in the back pocket of his trousers: the clip caught in the wool, so that, when he left the room, he unwittingly dragged the blanket after him. You might have thought that he would notice the weight, but he didn't, and it was only when he was on the landing outside that he realised what had happened. He left the blanket hanging on the banister. You might also have thought that the analyst would say something, if only to avoid liability for an accident on the stairs, but he must have been of Herman Galberg's sphingid ilk.

Galberg said he thought he could help me, but puzzlingly foretold that the cost of his relieving my anxieties would be a cooling of my passion for logical theory. Some years later both the anxieties and the passion had abated, but that hardly proved his thesis, and I was unable to test it more rigorously, for our first session was our last. There were two reasons for that: one, that he charged fifty pounds per hour (so the cooling passion was not the only cost), I was unemployed, this was 1979, and so these were old pounds; and two, that he died a week later.

Before doing so, he put me on to the Wrigley Clinic, which specialised in psychosexual disorders and gave free advice to deserving cases. On the way to my first appointment, I dropped into a nearby public gents for a pee and was innocently startled to find it as packed as the rush-hour Tube on which I had travelled. The place was a thriving gay rendezvous (aptly, it was in Swiss Cottage), its 'No

Loitering' sign scorned by its users – none of whom, apart from me, was peeing, and some of whom, perhaps, were also on their way to the clinic, for in those days homosexuality was still often regarded as an illness. At my college a gay and gloomy (if you're with me) student called Faber, known generally as Homo Faber, was subjected to electroconvulsive therapy for his gayness. Instead, it lifted his gloom, as well as clouding his memory.

In the waiting room of the clinic, I eyed the other patients and tried to guess their perversions, while they doubtless did the same to me. We all looked bland enough. The magazines on the table were the usual *Country Life* and *Punch* – has anyone other than a doctor or dentist ever bought these? – but a selection of cellophane-wrapped journals from a top shelf in Old Compton Street – *Dwarves on the Job*, say, or *Coprophile's Monthly* – might have shown greater consideration for our reading tastes.

I was rescued from the mutual eyeing by Howard Syme, a man of sallow hue and cheerless mien, with hair combed in barcode style over his bald patch. He greeted me laconically, in a thin and piping voice, and led me upstairs. When we entered his tiny and windowless room, the air was stale from the previous consultation and I noted that the pillow on the couch was still dented by the head of the preceding patient: at the corner there was a stray hair with a flake of dandruff attached. After some face-to-face formalities, Syme invited me to lie down, and, as he showed no intention of puffing up the pillow, I did so before making myself comfortable and starting to ramble. It is hard to conceive how therapists can bear listening to such stuff hour after hour. It may well be that Syme nodded off: as he was sitting behind my head, I couldn't tell. There was no sound of that slow and heavy breathing characteristic of the deep sleeper, but on the other hand he said nothing for tens of minutes. Winnicott, the famous analyst, wrote a case history of a patient whose defence mechanism was to fall asleep whenever a threatening topic arose: the report was peppered with 'Patient asleep now', and at one point Winnicott added 'I think I must have fallen asleep too.' It is pleasing to think of the two of them snoring away at someone's expense.

After a few of these near-monologues, I had become sensitive to Syme's slightest movement, and I could tell when the fifty minutes were nearly up by the faint rustling of his watch against his cuff. On the red-letter occasions when he did open his mouth, it was to chirp something irrelevant (perhaps, having momentarily woken up, he was confusing me with another patient), perplexing (as when he reproached me for speaking in grammatical sentences), or infuriating (he treated my every utterance as a symptom calling for explanation, rather than as an observation that might merit a reply).

The screen goes misty and wavy, on the soundtrack a harp plays rapid glissandos, and the tortured twenty-two-year-old of the sexual anxieties morphs into the burnt-out fifty-four-year-old of the kaleidoscopic symptoms. (The informed reader will recognise that we have progressed to the next of Erik H Erikson's psychosocial stages. In another couple of decades – I should live so long – I may describe the men and women who usher me through the final stage, that of senile despair.) Burnt-out Oliver is sitting in another waiting room, that of Glenda Gibbon, whom he has been told he is going to like very much. It now being 2011, he knows more about his therapist, for he has looked at her website, which has told him that before her psychological training she worked first in the theatre and then in catering. The precise nature of her jobs in those domains was not stated, but the implication was that they provided valuable grounding for her present occupation. The message of the waiting room, in which I sat alone, was that Glenda Gibbon was a very serious person, for there was no *Country Life* or *Punch* (the latter would have been at least nine years old, a good age even in a waiting room), let alone the other organs mentioned above – the only reading matter being a single copy of T S Eliot's *Notes Towards the Definition of Culture*.

Gibbon herself, a masculine person with Eton crop and laced boots, was at pains to reinforce the message, for her remarks were larded with highbrow references. 'Like Proust,' she said, 'you are a high-functioning neurasthenic.' I liked the high-functioning, but not the neurasthenic – an archaism suggesting that the training mentioned on her website had taken place in the nineteenth century – and was in two minds about the Proust. She may have carried on like that because I was a professor of philosophy, her mistaken premiss being that analytic philosophers are repositories of encyclopedic erudition, rather than the oikish technicians they so often are in fact. A frivolous Gibbon was detectable inside the pompous one, there being a ukulele propped against the sofa.

I was frustrated by her canine knack of spotting the wrong tree and barking up it. For a reason that escapes me, I mentioned Croydon, and she seemed to believe that the root of my misery might lie in that suburb. In fact Croydon makes me smile: I have never been there, save to pass through it on the train to Gatwick (not itself a smiling matter), but (1) it was pronounced Kyaydon by the man with the speech-impediment who was bizarrely employed to announce the stations, (2) the hamster which I owned and loved as a child came from there (my father confused me by saying that hamsters came from Syria, and sticking a poster of Aleppo above the cage so that it would feel at home) and (3) a pastoral in the *Oxford Book of Sixteenth Century Verse* contains Croydon where Corydon should be.

Her prediction of my liking for Glenda Gibbon having been refuted, Vera now referred me to Dr Alison Whish, a psychiatrist. I don't have a firm grasp of the distinctions between psychiatrists, psychologists and psychotherapists, but I believe I have just listed them in descending order of status. Whish had high status even among her species, for she was a senior consultant, operating (in the non-surgical sense) from a private mental hospital. When I arrived there for our first consultation, there was a rigmarole at the front door, the porter needing to ensure that, when a visitor entered, none of the inmates exited. These were largely drug-addicts and, as confirmed by skeletal appearances, anorexics: it would have been a waste of everyone's time if they had been allowed to slip out for, respectively, some crack or a laxative.

Whish's grandeur was not reflected in her consulting room, which was as poky and stuffy as Howard Syme's had been all those years ago, its only advantage over Syme's being that it had a window, which Whish flung open as I entered. Doubtless the intended effect was to admit oxygen, but the actual one was to admit the carbon monoxide and din of the passing traffic. Whish's appearance was similarly incongruous. I had expected a severe, intellectual-looking type of a certain age, along the lines of Virginia Woolf in her last years, but the resemblance was closer to Diana Dors in her *beaux jours*: Whish's jersey hugged her ample breasts, her tights rustled as she crossed and uncrossed her legs, and, when the legs were crossed, a shoe dangled tantalisingly from her toe. Such diversions are fine in their place, but are not helpful when you're feeling brittle.

Whish was clearly bored as I shouted my symptoms over the roar of the buses – I caught her glancing at her Blackberry – but her ears pricked up when I told her that I was contemplating suicide. She asked me whether I had ever thought about methods. 'Not only have I thought about them,' I replied, 'I have a precisely worked-out plan.' That was an overstatement, but I had a pretty good idea, for I had spent some time considering the matter. The three desiderata, it seems to me, are ease, certainty and painlessness. They are hard to combine.

Buying rat poison is easy, and swallowing enough of it will certainly kill you, but you will suffer on the way. Injecting a large dose of morphine is certain and painless, but the stuff is hard to get. Taking painkillers with alcohol is easy and painless, but may not finish you off. A method I had heard recommended was to don thin clothes, climb a cold mountain, drink half a bottle of whisky and wait for hypothermia to set in. The obvious drawback was the bore of getting to, and up, the mountain. It then occurred to me that the mountain could be replaced by a capacious deep-freeze, easily buyable from Peter Jones, so one day I went to the kitchen department there to take some measurements. My wife accompanied me and held the end of the tape-measure: I was glad of her help, but disconcerted by her enthusiasm for the project. None of the freezers in the shop was large enough for comfort, but the assistant told me that much bigger ones were available online and could be delivered in a couple of days. I didn't place an order, but was reassured by the knowledge that, if and when the time came, I had a method that scored reasonably well on all three tests.

Whish wrote rapidly as I told her all this. When I had finished, she exclaimed 'I don't think I'll ever be able to go into Peter Jones's kitchen department again!' – an immoderate response from someone surely used to hearing confessions that were more lurid. In my stride, I went on to describe the time I had experimented with tying a plastic bag over my head. 'I don't know whether you've ever tried it,' I said. '*Of course* I haven't,' she cried. 'You *mustn't* normalise these things!' I had assumed that the psychiatrist's chair was meant for a full and frank expression of views, but I should have been more guarded. That was brought home to me when I later saw Whish's report to Vera: 'On balance,' it concluded, 'I have decided that he does not need to be certified.' This was closer to the wind than I had ever imagined sailing. It was cold comfort to read also that I was 'cognitively intact'.

In keeping with their high status, psychiatrists are loth to waste time in chat, so Whish dismissed me with a prescription for an antidepressant and a referral to one Michael Urmson for talking therapy. She told me that I would like him very much – clearly a standard phrase in this context, and one that I had learnt to take as a term of art. When I reached the front door of the hospital to leave, there was another rigmarole, the porter this time needing persuasion that I was not an inmate. I offered to eat one of his fig rolls to nail any suspicion of anorexia, but he remained stony-faced, and in any event I could think of no ready defence to a charge of drug-addiction. The impasse was ended by a call to Whish's secretary, who came to the porter's booth and confirmed, with little conviction, that I was sane enough to go. Perhaps Whish had already dictated her report and the secretary had noted the 'on balance' bit.

The antidepressant was Citalopram, which apparently is the usual first choice. I was chary of taking it because (a) I was not depressed, at least to my untutored introspection, (b) I didn't like to interfere with my brain, (c) I was frightened of the side effects and (d) I understood, from casual reading, that no one knew whether, which or why antidepressants worked. Nevertheless I gave the stuff a whirl and, as to (c), soon added grogginess, nausea and sweating to my other symptoms. I complained to Whish, who now plucked Prozac from her pharmacopoeia and told me to stick with it, as it could take six weeks for me to 'feel the benefit'. (I had last heard this homely formula forty-five years previously, when my great-aunt Edna had urged me to remove my coat indoors, so that I would feel the benefit when I went out again.) The side effects were even worse and, after six weeks with no benefit in sight, I decided to call it a day. When I phoned Whish to ask whether I should suddenly stop or gradually reduce the dose, her reply was strange: 'Oliver, you understand that, if you stop taking the medication, I'll have to tell your father.' This was the first time my father, dead for thirty-four years, had arisen in our conversation. I didn't press Whish on the point, but the following day I received from her a text message in which she confessed to having confused me with a teenage patient of the same name. I should have been relieved that only an antidepressant, and not (say) an amputation, was at stake.

Michael Urmson, the therapist to whom Whish referred me, had an opulent room with a cocktail cabinet, heavy drapery, various comfortable chairs, and a large mahogany sideboard bearing, among other things, silver-framed snaps of a young woman with some children and a labrador, all of them grinning. The room also contained *two* couches: why? I was struck by the contrast between this saloon and Whish's miserable box: perhaps Urmson was compensating for his lower status. The *mise-en-scène* may have been bogus, for such apartments are available on time-share, and the happy family in the photos may have belonged to another sharer.

Two doors betrayed strain behind the appearances. One was the door to the street: although the postal address was Harley Street, the number had an A after it, and the entrance, in an alley, had been built for tradesmen. The other was the door between Urmson's room and its antechamber. This small alcove contained Joyce, whom Urmson described as his secretary but who may have worked for many others as well. She was a seamless natterer down the phone, and the connecting door was so flimsy that, when closed, it allowed her soliloquies to waft into the consulting room: 'I said to Steve... new curtains for the lounge... Las Vegas this year... it was her bunions...' If I could hear Joyce, she could hear me – or would have if, for a moment, she had staunched her logorrhoea. Perhaps, therefore, it was in my interest to let it flow on, but it was so distracting that I asked Urmson to put his head round the door and request her to pipe down. The only effect of his request was that thereafter Joyce glared at me whenever I entered or left. She continued to natter while doing so.

Other infuriating noises were nearer at hand. Scattered among the consulting room's knick-knacks were six clocks, each with a loud tick. Either (i) this was a fetish of Urmson's which might itself have merited therapy (are psychotherapists like chiropodists, who can treat themselves, or like brain surgeons, who shouldn't?) or (ii) the idea was that Urmson could check the time when gazing in any direction, and thus without offending the patient by a glance at the watch. The combined racket reminded me of the 'At the Old Clockmaker's' track on the LP of sound effects that I had treasured as a boy: only the cuckoo was lacking (unless I was he). When I remonstrated, Urmson put all but one of the clocks in his briefcase. The remaining one – just beside my chair and thus visible to him by a flick of the eye (this supported hypothesis (ii)) – had a lame tick which on its own was more irritating than the preceding orchestra, but Urmson declared that the briefcase was now full, and I lacked the stamina to press him on the capacity of his cupboards and drawers.

Unlike his predecessors, Urmson was a cheery fellow, in the mould of George Formby (I wondered whether, like Glenda Gibbon, he had a uke), and was disposed to outbursts of laughter. These may have been part of a technique, but seemed genuine. It dawned on me after a few sessions that I was paying £155 an hour to entertain him, when the consideration should have been moving the other way. As the sessions were having no other discernible effect, I decided to stop them. When I told him so, his manner changed abruptly. He sternly asserted that we were reaching a crux at which painful facts about me would surface, that I was already half-aware of them, and that my superficially cool decision to stop was a mark of panic: unless I continued to work through my feelings, I couldn't hope to get better. It would take, he estimated, at least another ten meetings (= £1,550). Irked by this baloney, I dug my heels in and we parted frostily. It being our final encounter, I returned Joyce's glare as I left. On reaching home I found an email from Urmson, sent after my departure from his office: its heading was 'AVOIDANCE', but its only other content was a bill with a warning that legal action would be taken if I didn't pay within two weeks. I was lucky to shake him off so easily: a friend of mine only managed to get rid of her therapist by giving him her grand piano.

Antidepressants and talk having flopped, Whish was nearly out of ideas, but she suggested that I try a course of cognitive behavioural therapy, for which she recommended Dr Peter Spreadbridge. 'Do you think I'll like him?' I asked, and was disappointed to receive a vacant stare in return. In fact he was rather amiable – a man of about my age, with the appearance and demeanour of an old-school stockbroker, occasionally chortling and often calling me his dear chap. I would not have been surprised if he had offered me a snifter. Although cognitive behavioural therapy sounds dauntingly scientific, the treatment Spreadbridge provided consisted mainly of spouting anecdotes, few and often repeated, which he sprinkled with nuggets of advice that were either obvious (it's good to get some fresh air every day) or useless (don't dwell on your symptoms). I testily remarked that you might just as well encourage a man with a broken leg not to dwell on it: he'd still be in agony and unable to walk.

This provoked a chortle. Spreadbridge also pressed on me some volumes in a series of books called *Overcoming*_____, the blank being filled respectively by 'Depression', 'Panic', 'Binge Eating', and so on. The ones I glanced at appeared to have been written for the under-fives and, although they had different authors, all said the same things, in the vein of Spreadbridge's platitudes. It is a mark of the medieval state of psychiatry that CBT is one of the most enthusiastically promoted treatments. Auntie Edna could have done better.

After Spreadbridge I had had enough, so I staggered on by myself for a few months, at the end of which I felt even worse, physically and mentally. All physical tests having long been exhausted, I was fain to try further shrinkage. This time I went through the back door, consulting Roger Scoles, a friend who is a child psychiatrist. His wife is a psychogeriatrician, and no one else in their family covers the middle parts of the life-cycle (why 'cycle'?), but I had enough of the toddler in me for his opinion to be relevant. Delivered over a bacon sandwich in his local greasy spoon, it ran as follows: 'What rotten luck! You'll get better on your own, but who knows when? Psychiatry sometimes speeds things up a bit, but sometimes not. You can't tell.' For a man who had devoted his life to the subject, this was modest. From their crestfallen expressions, the attentively listening men in overalls and hi-vis jackets, who were drinking tea at neighbouring tables, seemed to think so too.

Roger told me that he had heard good reports of

a psychiatrist called William Porson, and so, mindful of Bruce and the spider, I made an appointment to see this man. At our first meeting it was clear that he confused psychiatric practice with lecturing on psychiatry, for instead of asking me about myself he held forth on the taxonomy of mental illness. 'In the old days,' he boomed, 'you'd have been described as having a nervous breakdown, but we don't talk in those terms any more. Nowadays we say that people have depression, or an anxiety disorder.' From his complacent smile it appeared that he took this to be progress, but to my ear the new terminology was as vague as the old – an impression reinforced when he added, the smug smile widening, 'Of course, everyone's depression is different.'

At the end of the meeting we repeated the routine I had gone through with Whish: Porson announced that he would give me an antidepressant and refer me to someone for talking therapy. I told him of my bad experience with Citalopram and Prozac, so he searched on his computer and came up with Seroquel. When I got home I googled this drug and read that it was used for schizophrenia and bipolar disorder, neither of which I was aware of having, and contraindicated in cases of cardiac arrhythmia, which, as I had told Porson, I did have. The list of possible side effects, even more alarming than usual, included: drooling; inability to move the eyes; lip smacking or puckering; rapid or wormlike movements of the tongue; sticking out of the tongue; shuffling walk; slurred speech; uncontrolled chewing movements; uncontrolled twisting movements of the neck, trunk, arms and legs; unusual facial expressions; and painful or prolonged erection of the penis. Reluctant to terrify family and friends, I dropped an email to Porson querying the prescription, and minutes later received a reply headed 'DO NOT TAKE SEROQUEL!' (The profession seem to favour capital letters for the subject box: cf. Urmson.) The message went on to explain that Porson had meant to prescribe Sertraline but had been cozened by the computer's predictive text. (They also seem to be absentminded: cf. Whish.) When I reported the incident to Roger, he gently asked 'Are you sure that Dr Porson didn't mean you to take Seroquel?' – leaving me to infer that Roger thought me psychotic.

Sertraline, although less malign than Seroquel, proved no more benign than the other antidepressants, so I gave it up after a few days and made an appointment with Joaquín Jiménez, to whom Porson had referred me for more talk. Jiménez, who had a room in a block called Marbles House, was a young man, and I meanly doubted that he had yet amassed the *Lebensweisheit* for a patient of my knowledge and experience. More troubling was his English: a thick Spanish accent made it hard to tell how good his grammar and lexicon were, and I found myself pressing my thoughts into noddy sentences – possibly causing him to think *my* English elementary. When he phoned my office, he threw my secretary by pronouncing the J of 'Joaquin' as a gutteral H. The message I received was 'A Mr Hawkins rang.'[1]

Jiménez began by asking what I hoped to get from our sessions, and I replied that I wanted to stop having the symptoms that had brought me to him. 'That's an unrealistic aim for therapy,' he rejoined. 'What would be a realistic aim?' I asked as mildly as I could, and his answer was to the effect that I might gain insight into my condition and thereby come to cope with it. I thought again of the man with the broken leg: he goes to the doctor to have it set, and the doctor says 'That's an unrealistic aim, but I'll give you some insight into your condition so that you can cope with it.' Not wishing to antagonise Jiménez at the start, I kept the thought to myself, leant back in my chair and began burbling again, as I had to all those who had gone before him.

A recurring theme of our conversations was my eagerness to impress people. Jiménez suggested that this was a source of stress, which might in turn explain my symptoms. I said that I had often thought of getting a cat, which would be hard to impress: if I tried to do so, the stress could increase, but I might abandon the attempt, in which case it could diminish. It was a feeble joke and I'm not sure that Jiménez got it. In response he mumbled some words which I think were 'Yes, you should get

---

[1] I once went to a party given by a clinical psychologist who worked at Guy's Hospital: many of the other guests were colleagues of hers, and I was surprised at how few of these spoke fluent English. Admittedly they worked for the NHS, which hoovers up foreign practitioners of all sorts, but you would think a good grasp of the language more important in this field than in, say, orthopaedics.

a cat,' but may have been 'No, do not get a cat.' I acted on the former interpretation, and now have a tabby who holds me in contempt. She is my only tangible benefit from psychotherapy.

Baby Jesus

The pet names that husbands and wives give to each other are usually sickening. I have been startled to hear a peevish codger address his battleaxe of a wife as Numsy. When replying, she called him Pumpkin. It is therefore with embarrassment that I admit to calling my wife Fluffy. I can't remember how it started, but the habit is now so deeply entrenched that we don't think about it. If I address her by her real name, it sounds stilted and she thinks I am telling her off. Even referring to her by it when talking to a third person makes me uncomfortable, but then so does calling her Fluffy: it's a lose-lose situation. Things are easier with our close friends, for they too know her by her nickname.

In return, Fluffy calls me Baby Jesus. I do remember how this started. It was at the passionate stage of our courtship, and we were in the four-poster bed (which we had christened Pat, after the postman) in my Barbican flat. An oak four-poster, let alone one with a large carved pineapple in its headboard and with strawberry-shaped finials, has no business in a brutalist concrete block where the ceiling clears the finials by one inch. My mother had bought it as a present when I got engaged to a predecessor of Fluffy's, a Chinese woman whose pet name at the time escapes me, but who has become known, since we acrimoniously split up, as The Peril. We had the bed in The Peril's house, and when I moved out of there and into the Barby I took it with me, leaving The P to sleep on the floor – for she had disposed of her previous bed to make room for Pat. I hope she got backache. Pat was a flimsy repro and, when you moved or turned over, the frame would rock and creak rhythmically, as if copulation were in progress. I was celibate for my first couple of years in the flat, but the noise was good for my cred with the neighbours.

It was that moment when, seed and passion spent, you used to light a cigarette, but, as neither Fluffy nor I smoked, she wrapped the duvet round my head and shoulders, like a shawl. 'Baby Jesus!' she cried. 'You look like Baby Jesus in the manger.' She told me to put on my spectacles, which were small, round and horn-rimmed. 'Now you look even more like Baby Jesus!' Then she made me get up and look at myself in the mirror. The resemblance eluded me: Baby Jesus didn't wear horn-rimmed specs, and the duvet made me look more like the Virgin Mary, if anyone. These awkward facts notwithstanding, the name stuck, although Fluffy now often shortens it to BJ – one of those pairs of initials that often do duty for names. JB is another, but some pairs are not so catchy: you seldom come across a person known as, say, MN. Linguists may be able to explain this, as they can such odd phenomena as the use of front-stressed disyllabic words to express disbelief: rubbish, bollocks, nonsense, or (archaically) gammon, for example. It's obvious, of course, why you don't find people called MS, VD or BO.

The thing has grown into a cult. Fluffy bought a Ladybird Book called *Baby Jesus* and put it on display in the lav, for visitors to leaf through while at stool, and last Christmas she snapped up, at the Spitalfields bric-à-brac market, a model nativity scene with ox and ass, two shepherds, three wise men, Mary and Joseph, and BJ with a nimbus – all in plastic. She set them out on our coffee table, but failed to put them away on Twelfth Night. Nine months later they are still there, covered in dust which our Polish cleaner ignores; a devout Catholic, she may think it sacrilegious to touch them. In the intervening period the arrangement has been disturbed, so that Baby Jesus is no longer the centre of the other figures' attention: one of the shepherds has fallen on his front, and the black wise man is examining the ox's bottom.

As in Fluffy's case, some of our friends know me by my nickname – one of them, a historian of ecclesiastical art, calling me *The* Baby Jesus – and I am so used to it that I apply it to myself. 'It's Baby Jesus,' I called into the entryphone in the street outside a friend's flat. Passers-by looked twice.

Our household is too shambolic for us to manage a weekly shopping expedition, but when the fridge is empty we make an emergency sortie to Waitrose to relieve immediate needs. Recently, when we were there, Fluffy wandered down an aisle and called to me from the far end: 'Baby Jesus, come and look at these beans – they're on special.' (I wish she wouldn't use that phrase.) A small boy, aged about four, who was walking past with his mother, stopped and pointed up at me, wonderstruck. 'It's Baby Jesus!' he gasped. I smiled down at him. His mother looked uncomfortable. 'It's not really Baby Jesus,' she said. Fluffy, returning from her inspection of the beans, irresponsibly interjected 'Oh yes, this is the real Baby Jesus all right.' The mother grabbed the hand of the child and pulled him away, shaking her head and saying 'I don't want to get involved'; but the damage had been done and, as we continued our shopping, we could hear him prattling away, the words 'Baby Jesus' ringing out over the shelves every few seconds. Our routes crossed again by a spillage that had been marked off, like roadworks, with rubber cones. The boy, by now in a lather, pointed at me again, seized one of the cones, put it to his mouth like a megaphone and shouted 'BABY JESUS!' down it. Other shoppers turned and stared. I beamed at them. Let us hope that his scripture teacher sorted him out.

DIE – DIY

When it was clear that my mother had only a few days to live, my wife Fluffy phoned several undertakers for quotes. Having looked in *Which?*, she rang only those who had been highly recommended. To her surprise, all the people she spoke to sounded rough and all responded in the same way: they would not engage until there was a dead body. Perhaps this was a way of avoiding cries of Wolf, but we thought it more likely that they wanted to maximise their bargaining strength: in the first place, once the person has died, there is a need to move quickly, for hospital mortuaries are crowded and room needs to be made for new arrivals; in the second, the newly bereaved are too distraught to haggle vigorously. Once my mother had died, Fluffy called the undertakers again, and again their responses were alike, the terms they quoted being uniformly astronomical. Even for the basic service of driving the body from mortuary to crematorium they wanted many hundreds of pounds.

Being a competition lawyer, I thought I sniffed a cartel, and I remembered that years previously the Monopolies and Mergers Commission had investigated concerns about a lack of competition in the sector. My firm acted in the case, the lawyers enjoying feeble puns about horizontal mergers, black-box decisions, RIP-offs, and the like.

Disgusted, Fluffy decided to run my mother's funeral herself. She did so because she is kind, enterprising and practical, not because I was too grief-stricken to lift a finger; on the contrary, I was relieved, for my mother had been senile and depressed for the preceding decade, and in her final year had been rotting in an NHS psychogeriatric unit called Ash House. When we inspected her in the mortuary, I was curious rather than upset: she was lying, covered by a purple cloth, on a table – her mouth ajar, her head lolling slightly to one side – and I was struck by the chilled-blancmange feel of her cheek. As a child I had adored her and often reflected that her dying would be the worst thing that could happen to me. Now here I was at age forty-eight, her death leaving me as cold figuratively as her cheek was literally. No doubt there's a moral – perhaps that whatever matters greatly to you now won't matter so much to you later. Some would add that you therefore shouldn't let it matter greatly now, but the inference is problematic.

Fluffy and I had just bought a house, which we were doing up, and so the place was full of Poles, including a joiner whom his colleagues called Earache. The cotton wool in his ear may have been relevant, but we took it that they were just saying

'Eric' in a Polish way. Fluffy asked Eric whether he would knock up a coffin for my mother. He had not made one before, but agreed to have a go, and asked how big my mother was. 'My size or a bit smaller,' said Fluffy, so he took her measurements and, when the thing was nearly ready, asked her to try it for size. She was uncomfortable about this, just as the able-bodied are reluctant to sit in wheelchairs.[1] The size test having been passed, Eric sanded down the coffin, and Fluffy then decorated its inside with photographs, letters, and messages such as 'We love you Mummy Black' (marginally better than 'Bye Bye Nan', which I once saw.)

As the coffin would not fit into our Honda Jazz, Eric lent us his bright orange Volvo Estate for the day of the cremation. The Volvo was old, and much scuffed from the incidents of joinery, but he gallantly washed and polished it, and attached some black ribbons to the wing mirrors. With one of the back seats folded down, the coffin slid in snugly. We set out early, for we were due at the crematorium at eight-thirty a.m., Fluffy having booked the first slot of the day in order for us to enjoy the reduced rate that applied at times of low demand. Our first stop was to pick up her mother (Mummy Geddes), who enjoyed an outing, and our second one was at the mortuary, where, squeamish about handling the body,

---

[1] I did so at Inverness airport when I was waiting for a flight to London, there being no other seats free, and received sharp looks from other passengers. They were worth enduring, once I realised that the EasyJet plane on the tarmac was already full and was going to fly to London and back before it took us on board.

we tipped a couple of porters to lift it into the coffin. Off we then went to the crem, with Fluffy driving, Mummy Geddes in the front passenger seat, and me sitting behind, next to the front end of Mummy Black. I now realised that the coffin had a design flaw: although the lid had a lip, it was not fastened down, and it rattled whenever we went over a bump. Time being tight, Fluffy was driving much more quickly than is customary on such occasions; if we went over a sleeping policeman, the lid might fly off, and if the jolt were hard enough – my imagination was off the leash – we would have a Paddy Dignam situation, with the back door of the car springing open, the lidless coffin tumbling out, and Mummy B rolling from it on to the tarmac, exposed, if not exactly vulnerable, to the rush-hour traffic. I kept my elbow pressed on the lid throughout the journey.

We arrived at the crematorium just as the doors were opening. Fluffy asked the two attendants on duty, Eamonn and Larry, to help us carry the coffin to what she called the catapult. This caused confusion till they realised that she meant 'catafalque' (she was new to the jargon). There were just the five, or six, of us present, for there was to be no service: we had decided to separate the burning from the rite of passage, which was to be a tree-planting-cum-ash-scattering at a later date. Eamonn and Larry showed no surprise at the absence of ceremony. Eamonn told us that sometimes the deceased's family delegate the whole thing to undertakers and later receive the ashes by post; in those circumstances, he said, a reputable undertaker will, as a mark of respect, sit in the crematorium with the body for a quarter of an hour before it is burnt. Having decided to use other means of showing our respect for Mummy B, who was now lying on the catapult – actually a conveyor belt – in front of a sliding door, we asked Eamonn to commence proceedings. Like an automated call centre, he offered us three options: (1) the coffin stays put while we leave; (2) the door slides open and we watch the coffin pass through; (3) a curtain surrounds the coffin, which then moves unseen. We plumped for (2), which Eamonn brought about with a discreet press of a button on the wall near his hip. The belt moved smoothly and silently, but the door sprang open and slammed shut, like that of a cuckoo clock.

We were about to leave when Eamonn asked whether we would like to see what happened next. He was a cheery man, with the manner of a family butcher, and contrasted with the morose and sallow Larry, who seemed better suited to his job. Having assented, we were led behind the scenes and found ourselves again standing by the coffin, which had come to a stop just the other side of the cuckoo-clock door. I had assumed that it would be propelled directly into the furnace, but the operation turned out to be lower-tech than that. Eamonn and Larry heaved the coffin off the conveyor belt and dragged it along a corridor with tiled walls. Their manner had changed from obsequious (in both senses) to brutish – doubtless from habit, this being a part of the building into which they were not usually followed by mourners. Chatting and whistling, they manhandled the coffin as if it were a crate of bananas, finally dropping it with a thud on the floor of a large room which at first glance looked like a launderette. The bank of spin dryers in the wall was in fact a bank of furnaces, including an extra-large one for outsized bodies. 'We use this one more and more,' Eamonn said, 'what with people getting taller and fatter. Soon you'll need to be a weightlifter to do our job.' He and Larry emitted loud laughs – Eamonn's genuine, Larry's forced – and I pictured my mother's tiny, frail body in the coffin, on which Larry was now resting his foot. They then yanked the coffin into one of the regular furnaces, and Eamonn slammed the door and turned on the heat. 'There's a peephole in the front, so you can see how she's cooking,' he pointed out, and invited me to look through. I declined, for I had heard that a corpse, when it reaches a certain temperature, will suddenly sit up, and I didn't relish the prospect of my mother staring back at me through the flames, her mouth still ajar.

Another false assumption I had made was that we could take her ashes home with us, but it takes some time to incinerate a body, and then the remains have to cool down. They also need to be pulverised, for what comes out of the furnace is not a fine powder, but a mixture of ash, clinker, bone and incombustible material such as prosthetic hip joints and tooth fillings. Eamonn pointed to a heap of incombustibles in a large yellow plastic tub, of the kind used by builders for small rubble. I thought of Belsen. Once these have been separated, the rest is put into the pulveriser – a drum in which a ball whizzes round. We refused the offer of a demonstration. Two days later we returned to collect my mother's ashes. Larry, who was on duty alone, handed us a cellophane sack of pale grey powder. 'How do we know that they're *her* ashes?' I asked. He smiled with his mouth only, and said nothing.

The planting of the memorial tree took place in Kensington Gardens, as my family had lived near there for many years. The Gardens charge a high price for the right to plant; in my view, the money should flow the other way, for the result is that they gain an extra tree. It was a small gathering, most of my mother's friends being either dead or too doddery to attend. Before her own decline, my mother had been strikingly casual about that of her friends: 'They're all gaga or dead,' she would laughingly remark. Was she stoical or heartless? Then, of course, she went gaga, and then she died. Few of those present at the ceremony looked as if they could stand for long, so I greeted them briefly and we moved quickly on to the planting. A gardener had dug a hole and was standing by it with the tree. My idea was to empty my mother's ashes into the hole before the tree went in, but the gardener warned me to use only a trowelful and to sprinkle from a crouching position, because ashes (a) were bad for trees – even ash trees, such as the one he was guarding – and (b) tended to blow into people's faces. I followed his instructions, but still got some of my mother in my eyes, it being a breezy day. The ashes smelt like fertiliser, notwithstanding (a). Once the tree was in, I read Fidele's dirge: it is hackneyed, but my mother had loved it and it was, as they say, what she would have wanted. It is also a dialogue, but I read both parts – just as I had once said the lines of both Rosencrantz and Guildenstern in a student production of *Hamlet*.[2] We were all about to shuffle on to the orangery for tea when Precious, my mother's quondam carer, asked if she too could read something. I couldn't forbid it, and so the ceremony was rounded off with some doggerel of the Clinton's Cards variety, only much longer. She may have written it herself.

Kensington Gardens don't allow you to mark the tree, so, if you want to visit later, you have to remember what it looks like. That proved to be a problem, for I am hopeless at tree-spotting: I can manage an oak and a Christmas tree, but an ash is beyond my power. Nevertheless I was confident of identifying my mother's tree, because I could remember roughly where it was and the other trees in the neighbourhood were much bigger. I was therefore baffled when, a couple of years after the planting, I returned to find only a cluster of tall, mature trees: either my mother's had shot up, or it had died and been quietly removed. Fluffy and I had a similar experience when she took me to see her father's tree in Richmond Park, which has the same no-plaque policy. A few yards from the tree to which Fluffy had led me, a woman was talking to another

---

[2] The man playing Guildenstern proved to be useless, and the director thought of replacing him with a dog; but (1) we didn't have one and (2) dogs, simply by not acting, steal the show. A stage dog I recently saw created mayhem by barking at an audience member who had an odd laugh.

tree. Assuming that this person was a nutter, I tried to avoid her gaze, but she then called out to us: it was Roz, Fluffy's stepmother, who told us that we had got the wrong tree. Fluffy retorted that it was Roz who had the wrong one. There was a tense standoff. It would save bother if parks allowed memorial trees to be marked; they allow the marking of memorial benches, so their policy is inconsistent.

After the planting of my mother's tree, we had to decide what to do with the rest of her ashes – i.e. almost all of them. Precious told me that my mother had said she wanted them scattered over Bidston Hill, in Birkenhead, where she had spent her childhood; but we needed somewhere to store them meanwhile. The chosen vessel was a large Lipton Yellow Label tea tin: Fluffy put the sack inside, wrote 'MUMMY BLACK XXXXXX' in felt tip on the front of the tin, and then placed the tin, with a plastic tiara on top, on a shelf of our kitchen dresser. Nine years later it is still there, for I haven't got round to traipsing up to Birkenhead. In the meantime Mummy Geddes has died, and her ashes are in a Brooke Bond Red Label tin, similarly marked but without a tiara, on the same dresser. One morning I found that Fluffy had slyly moved Mummy B's tiara on to Mummy G's tin. I slyly moved it back again and, the next morning, found that it was back on Mummy G. Over a week it went back and forth – Fluffy and I saying nothing to each other about it – but eventually Fluffy gave up, and the tiara remains on Mummy B. One way in which both Mummies could enjoy it would be to mix them up and keep them in the same tin. I suggested this as a space-saving expedient – it was better to avoid mentioning the tiara – and speculated that the effect might be pleasing: as Mummy G's ashes are darker than Mummy B's (Mummy G was Spanish), we could create swirly patterns, as some people do with sand in bottles used as lamp stands. Fluffy found the idea distasteful.

On another morning I found our friend Cath, who had stayed the night and was helping herself to breakfast, peering into Mummy G's tin. 'This isn't Red Label,' she said; 'what have you got in here?' 'It's a rare Mongolian herbal brew,' I replied, and urged her to try some. It was a puerile joke and, when Fluffy intervened in the nick of time, Cath was appalled – not only by the joke but by the fact of our storing the Mummies on the dresser. It showed disrespect, she said. Neither Fluffy nor I could see what was wrong with having them so handy: in theory, we are fondly reminded of them at every mealtime, although in practice they have merged with the plates, the cups and the toast rack.

The dresser bears a third tea tin, currently empty, which Fluffy says is for me. My view is that this shows unseemly haste – I'm middle-aged and in fairly good health – and possibly also an ugly desire. I told her that there was no need for a tin, as I would be donating my body for medical research, but she ruled this out on the ground that the hospital sends the mangled corpse back to the family once the medical students have finished throwing bits of it around the lab: she would not have a DHL man dumping a pile of squashy bin-liners on the doorstep and leaving her to sort through my organs – and these would anyway need to be cremated, in which case the tin would still be necessary. She had found it, she said, in the local bric-à-brac market and snapped it up because it was so quaint – Edwardian, the vendor told her. The truth is that it's merely shabby, with so much rust that (i) you can't tell the colour of the tea's label and (ii) there is no room to write 'OLIVER XXXXXX' in felt tip. Also on sale in the market was an urn already containing the ashes of a Mr Tooth. Fluffy was in two minds about this: on the one hand, it was sad to see Mr T abandoned on a stall; on the other, it seemed flippant to appropriate him as a knick-knack. I vetoed adding him to the collection.

One reason why I agreed to a DIY funeral and memorial ceremony for my mother was that I had bad memories of the conventional arrangements on the death of my father.[3] On the way to the crematorium, the driver of the hearse wound down his window to shout a greeting to a friend, and the service at the crem was perfunctory, the vicar on duty giving an all-purpose address that failed to include my father's name, which he probably didn't know. The duty organist then mangled some Bach, at one point losing his way and lurching into what sounded like 'Ain't Misbehavin'.

[3] Its year and month – 1977, August – could have been predicted from his pass for the British Museum Reading Room: the card bore a photo of his face and said merely 'Misha Black. Expires August 1977.' Later I had a similar card which said 'Oliver Black. Expires January 1985.' I became nervous as the date approached.

Weeks later there was a grand memorial service, taken by the Reverend Edgar Bowell, who lived in the flat two floors below us. A High Anglican, he had camp inclinations, enjoying bells, smoke and flamboyant costume. For the service he donned a flowing cloak in a shade of purple to which I doubt his clerical rank entitled him. I too hammed things up (I was a bumptious undergraduate at the time), thundering from the pulpit 'Death be not proud' as if it were Henry V's speech at Agincourt, and getting so carried away that at the end I forgot Bowell's warning to turn off the microphone. This caused agonising feedback when the music started. As I made a show of being musically sophisticated, my mother had left the selection to me. There was no need to consider what my father 'would have wanted', for he had been cloth-eared.[4] Determined to compensate for the pitiful performance at the crematorium, and deciding that something challenging was in order, I settled with the church's musical director on an *a cappella* work by Ives and an organ extravaganza by Messiaen. It was too clever by seven-eighths. Both tenors in the small choir were down with a bug, so that one line of the Ives was not sung (I didn't notice, and I'm sure no one else in the congregation did); and the Messiaen, a piece that demanded oomph, was too much for the eighteenth-century organ, which shook and wheezed. 'Why on earth did they have that ghastly din? A bit of Bach would have been so much more uplifting,' an

---

[4] Once, when he had been invited on to *Woman's Hour*, he was told that he would be asked to choose a piece of music. My mother did the job for him, picking a song called 'Ciao Ciao Bambina' which she liked.

old lady exclaimed to me as she left the church. Similar comments were widespread.

After the service, my mother and I had lunch with Bowell in his flat, which he occupied with a Romanian housekeeper, a fluffy white cat called Mr O'Grady, and two parrots, one of which whistled and the other said 'Amen' in Bowell's voice. Mr O'Grady would gaze menacingly at the parrots, but they looked big and fierce enough to repel an attack. They were not caged, and swooped down the corridor towards us as we walked to the dining room. We ducked, my mother toppling on to her knees. Throughout the meal Bowell called me Bruce, I don't know why: it may have been the name of the young man, a bit like me only more fey, whom we saw a few evenings later having an intimate supper with him at our local Chinese. On that occasion Bowell was dressed cap-à-pie in clinging leather, and seemed embarrassed to be spotted in such attire and company. My mother and I stopped at their table and greeted them warmly, but he looked straight through us.

Some weeks after that, Bowell too lost a member of the family, as my mother discovered by reading, in the deaths column of *The Times*, 'Mr O'Grady of Smallbone Mansions. Suddenly. No flowers please. Funeral from Battersea Bridge.' Our concierge filled in the details. Believing that Mr O'G needed fresh air and exercise, Bowell would toss him out of the front door of the block every morning. On the fateful day, the toss was too vigorous and propelled the cat under the wheels of a passing taxi. 'Funeral from Battersea Bridge' probably meant that he was going to cast the squashed remains into the river. Had we known earlier of Bowell's casual attitude to last rites, we might not have put him in charge of my father's memorial service. In any case, it should not have been held in a church, for my father was Jewish.

Our next DIY funeral was that of Mummy Geddes. She was the only person I have ever seen die, both my parents having gone while I was away from the bedside. Fluffy and I sat by Mummy G as her breathing became increasingly laboured, and, when it stopped, Fluffy passed her hand over Mummy G's eyes to close them. Mummy G then started breathing again, opened one eye, and gave Fluffy an old-fashioned look. This happened twice more, before the breathing stopped for good.

Eric could not make the coffin, for he too had died, shortly after finishing our house. Fluffy, an interior designer, asked the joiner on her current project to produce one, but he had scruples, and so we ended up using Dave, a local man, known for saying of everything that 'it's a nightmare'. Possibly this job really gave him nightmares. Fluffy brought the coffin home to decorate, and for that purpose laid it on the dining table. The windows of our dining room give straight on to the street, and we received alarmed looks from passers-by. Mummy G's coffin was given the works, the outside painted in Farrow & Ball's Hague Blue, with golden piping, and the inside lined with a luxurious silk that had been bought for curtains in Mummy G's flat. Now it was curtains in the other sense. When the decoration was complete, we put the coffin under the table, deciding not to mention it to the friends we were having to dinner that evening; but one of them banged her toe on it, and so an explanation was necessary. After that, the conversation flagged.

On the day before the cremation, Fluffy confected an extravagant wreath, copying an expert on YouTube. When I saw that it included lilies, I made a fuss, for I had heard that lilies were deadly to cats, and our cat Maud was sitting in the coffin, watching Fluffy at work. I couldn't face another funeral so soon, and Maud's would take some planning: she certainly was not going to follow Mr O'Grady over the side of Battersea Bridge. Fluffy flared up, claiming that the cat meant more to me than her mother did. The claim was true, but I couldn't admit it, so I retorted crisply that, while there was nothing we could do to revive Mummy G, we could at least keep Maud going by removing dangerous and inessential flora. The compromise we reached was that Maud would be evicted from the coffin and put in the top bedroom until the wreath was finished, and that the wreath would then be kept in the back yard overnight.

The manufacture of the wreath kept Fluffy up late, and the following morning, when we drove off to collect the body, she was too bleary, and I was too vague, to notice that we had left the front door of the house wide open. It stayed that way till our return in the late afternoon, but nothing was stolen. (Dwellers in the sticks sometimes smugly say 'In our village you can leave your front door unlocked and no one will rob you.' Well, the same is true in Tower Hamlets: put that in your clay pipe and smoke it.) Eric's Volvo Estate not being available, we had borrowed a newer and smarter one from our friend Penelope, who had previously lent it to others for the same purpose. 'I'm always happy to do so,' she tinkled, 'because I get it washed and polished for free.' I stopped myself from replying that Eric had washed and polished his Volvo before lending it to us. Eric was a kind, dignified and gentlemanly man. Fluffy, who loved him, sobbed loudly at his death. The sobbing took place in the bath, while I was standing at the basin shaving, and I was annoyed by the racket. There may have been a touch of jealousy in my surliness.

To ensure that we didn't scratch Penelope's car when we slid the coffin in, we laid two pieces of dowelling on the floor to serve as rollers. I had bought these from the local hardware shop and had offered the assistant £1,000 if he could guess why I wanted them. He looked uncomfortable when I told him. Mindful of the problem with Mummy Black's coffin, Fluffy had asked Dave to include screws for the lid of Mummy Geddes's, but this time there was a different design flaw: the coffin was made of MDF and hence very heavy, so we had to enlist a passer-by to help us get it into the car. Strangers can be obliging. There was a related problem with the handles, which were made of rope held in place by knots. Fluffy had sent me to buy the rope at a sailing and tackle shop, where I was baffled by the variety on offer. The assistant (who failed to smile when I tried to warm him up with a joke, no doubt familiar to him, about wedding tackle) told me that synthetic fibre was the strongest; but the synthetic ropes were all in lurid colours that would have clashed with the Hague Blue, so I settled for a traditional hemp. It was thick and inflexible, and Fluffy had trouble tying it; she had a knots badge from the Brownies, but was rusty, and the knots she produced were clumsy. A friend who had been in the merchant navy had a go, but his knots were even more amateurish, so we went back to Fluffy's and hoped that they would not unravel under the coffin's weight, to which the insertion of Mummy G's body made little difference, proportionately speaking. At the crematorium I was one of four bearers, the others being Eamonn and Larry – who both greeted us as old chums – and Fluffy's brother. Even though they were burly men, they clearly found the coffin a strain (I remembered Eamonn's quip about weightlifters), and I, a weed, nearly dropped my corner halfway down the aisle. How those soldiers manage the lead-lined jobs at state and ceremonial funerals, I have no idea.[5]

---

[5] I have been peripherally involved in three such funerals. One was Churchill's, during which my friend Adam and I, both aged eight, stood at attention by the telly until we got fed up with the droning of Richard Dimbleby. The second was that of the last pope but (I think) three, whose body, lying in state, I encountered when visiting St Peter's. He must have had a touch of the Zossimas, for there were two large extractor fans nearby and one of the halberdiers on guard had a wrinkled nose. I coveted the pope's shiny yellow shoes, and checked an impulse to whip them off his feet. Had I succumbed, and the halberdiers challenged me, I suppose I could have pleaded a desire to kiss the papal toe.
The third grand funeral was Princess Diana's, at the end of which she was driven up the M1 for burial at Althorp. I happened to drive up the same road a couple of hours earlier, on my way to visit friends in

At the time of her death, Mummy Geddes had a flat in a sheltered block for the elderly. As she had been friendly with many of her neighbours, Fluffy arranged for the cremation to be followed by a buffet lunch in the common room. Over the funeral baked meats, I chatted to a lady who turned out to be the mother of the actor who had played Nigel Pargetter in *The Archers*. Nigel had recently fallen to his death from the roof of Lower Loxley, so I said 'I understand that you too have recently suffered a loss – a fictional one, that is.' I went on to mention the facts, well known to addicts of the series, and doubtless to my interlocutor, that Nigel's scream was implausibly long – more appropriate to a fall from a skyscraper than to one from a manor house – and that it was now available as a ringtone. Mrs Pargetter, or whatever her name was, found none of

Nottinghamshire. The carriageway was almost empty, but the bridges and service stations were packed with mourners holding placards that bore messages such as 'Heaven Has One More Angel Now'. I gave a dignified wave as I sped past. By the time I left the motorway I was almost out of petrol; the first garage I found had cones across the entrance, and a sign saying 'Closed for two hours due to rispect', but as the need was urgent I drove between the cones and made to fill up. No petrol came out of the nozzle, so I went to the window to complain to the attendant, who was filing her nails. Continuing to do so, she asked me whether I couldn't read. I countered with animadversions on humbug, sentimentality and the Nuremberg Rally effect; she came back with something about smart-arses who had no respect; I told her that she couldn't even spell 'respect' and that I'd report her to the Cones Hotline; then I drove away with the petrol gauge still on E. I might have got further with grovelling and supplication, but my supply of self-control in matters Di-related had been exhausted the previous evening, when I had attended a concert at the Albert Hall and the music had been drowned by helicopters hovering over the mourners in Kensington Gore.

this amusing. She coldly said that *The Archers* was drivel, that she never listened to it, and that her son was bitter about having been written out of the plot. The last point surprised me, for I had assumed that the actor's departure had caused the character's death, rather than vice versa. Although a bit of a wally, Nigel seemed jovial enough to be kept alive.[6]

Conversation with Mrs P having cratered, I approached a lady who introduced herself as Egidia. She looked well into her nineties, but was smartly turned out and had a twinkle in her eye. 'The trouble with this place,' she drawled, 'is that everyone's so *old*. We need young blood.' I didn't reply that she was not one to talk, or that, if she enjoyed young company, she would do better to live somewhere else, for her complaint, rightly interpreted, was sensible enough: most of the people in the building were over eighty, but the threshold for admission was only fifty-five, and the place might have been livelier if there had been more residents at the lower end of the range. At the time, I was just under the threshold, and I thought of asking Fluffy whether we might keep the flat, for it was tempting to move in as soon as I qualified: everything was convenient, and a kindly

---

[6] She was right that *The Archers* is drivel, and I loathe myself for having followed it for over forty years, and for feeling a thrill when, as on that occasion, my life intersects events in Ambridge. The most thrilling moment occurred when Fluffy and I were giving a birthday party to a friend who knows Amy Shindler, the woman who plays Brenda Tucker. When guests started to arrive, I was still getting dressed, listening to *The Archers* while doing so. I turned the radio off while Brenda was speaking, and, as I walked downstairs, I heard her real voice wafting up from the floor below. Only the lack of the Mummerset accent preserved my grasp on reality.

warden kept an eye on you. I didn't pursue the matter, for the flat was small, the echoing tellies of the other residents would have got on my nerves, and, Fluffy being ten years younger than I, the rules might have required me to leave her behind.

Egidia perked up when she caught sight of three small women in hijabs at the other end of the room. One of them had been a patient in the bed next to Mummy G during the latter's terminal stay in hospital; the others were the sister and mother of the first. 'Ha ha – look at those funny little Muslims!' Egidia cried, as if they were miniature goats in a petting zoo. The three didn't notice, but various other guests glared at me, seeming to think that I was in charge of Egidia.

Finding that she had a flair for organising funerals, Fluffy offered her services when our friend George told us that Lena, his mother, had died. Lena had not looked after herself: a votary of alcohol, red meat and sticky puddings, she had reached fifteen stone when her health collapsed. The first hammer-blow was the onset of diabetes; the second, the resultant amputation of one leg; and thereafter her organs shut down one by one. The family gladly accepted Fluffy's offer, but insisted on a 'real' coffin, so Fluffy phoned some undertakers for quotes. She was greeted with the united bloody-mindedness that she had encountered when calling about Mummy Black: they would provide a coffin only as part of a complete funeral package. (We competition lawyers call it 'bundling'.) Fluffy turned to eBay and picked one up for £120. When she phoned the seller, a retired undertaker in Giggleswick, he told her that it had never been used – a point she had taken for granted – and that it had an 'oak effect' finish. 'Effect' sounding an alarm, Fluffy asked what it was really made of. MDF was the answer. Here was a problem in store, for an MDF coffin had nearly caused hernias with the featherlike Mummy Geddes inside, and Lena probably still topped thirteen stone without the leg. When Fluffy raised this concern, the ex-undertaker replied 'I could do you a cardboard one for fifty quid, but your lady might fall through the bottom of it while you're carrying her in.' He reinforced the warning by telling her that cardboard coffins go soggy if left in the rain. Fluffy stuck with the MDF.

As with our Mummies, only more so, Fluffy was keen to delegate the transferring of the body into the coffin, so she phoned the mortuary to arrange for porters to be on hand for that purpose. When she, George and I arrived, the duty manager, Derek, announced that the porters were on their break and that we would therefore have to help him with the body – a euphemism, it turned out, for lifting it ourselves. The fridge for the corpses comprised a stack of long drawers, like an office filing cabinet. Derek casually pulled open one of these to reveal a body bag no more than three feet long. My first thought was that Lena's other leg had also been amputated, but the bag was too small to have contained even her upper half: was the occupant a dwarf? 'Oops,' said Derek. 'Toddler: gored by a ram.

45

Not pretty.' He now squatted on his haunches and peered more carefully at the labels on the cabinet. 'Aha, here's *your* baby,' he said, opening a drawer that contained a bag of the right size. 'Better be sure, though.' He drew down the zip to reveal Lena's face: the flesh had tightened, pulling the mouth into a rictus that revealed teeth and gums. 'I'll leave you to it, then,' Derek called as he hurried towards the door. 'Have to get back to my post.' He had left the zip undone. Fluffy pulled it up, her eyes averted.

None of us wanting to touch Lena even through the bag, which was of thin plastic, we tried to lift her by clutching its corners, but could not gain a purchase; so George and I felt our way under her armpits, and Fluffy grabbed her ankle. George's face was almost as grey as Lena's, and a tear was rolling down his cheek, but he assured us that he was up to the job. On a count of three, we hauled Lena on to the edge of the drawer and then rolled her forward so that she slumped into the coffin a couple of feet below. So far as we could tell through the bag, her hips were in, but were wedged at an angle, and a lot of her sprawled over the rim. Further pushing and tugging caused her to fart, which made us jump, but we failed to squeeze all of her in or to get her to lie flat. Fluffy went to find Derek and returned with two porters, back from their elevenses. 'You go and wait at reception while we sort this dearie out,' one of them said wearily.

The sorting took over half an hour, which Derek – too busy, it seemed, to help with the body, but idle enough to chat – helped us to pass by telling us about what he called 'life at the mortuary'. Some of their corpses, he said, were fished from the Thames, some were never claimed by anyone, and one of the perks of the job was to keep the clothes of the unclaimed ones. He pointed to a camel hair coat, which had clearly never been in the Thames. 'Better than the charity shop,' he said, lighting a fag. 'Gosh, are you allowed to smoke here?' Fluffy asked. 'Doesn't worry our residents,' Derek replied. He then darted into his office and re-emerged with a large laminated chart, which he handed to her as a gift. The chart was divided into many small sections, each containing the name and the picture of a part of the anatomy, with some text underneath. Derek explained that the chart's purpose was to remind you of the evidence to look for when you were working out the cause of death. For example, in the section for fingertips, you were told to examine any material under the nail and to look for abrasions on the pad: if the person was found in the river, abrasions indicated that he or she had tried to grab on to something – which was evidence against suicide. 'You can't buy these charts, you know,' Derek said proudly. I tried to imagine one on display in an Athena shop.

He then withdrew again into his office, where he turned on Radio 1 and left us to listen to it through the partition, which was adorned with a photo of the Matterhorn (possibly in allusion to 'Über allen Gipfeln ist Ruh', but it seemed unlikely). When at last the porters came to tell us that all of Lena was in the coffin and ready to go, they were red and sweaty, as if they had spent the intervening time in the gym.

'How did you get her in?' I asked one of them, who responded with a mouth-only smile like the one Larry had given me when I had asked about Mummy Black's ashes. Fluffy whispered that they had probably broken Lena's arms and leg.

With three funerals under her belt, Fluffy now started talking of going into the business. After the experience with Lena, she was clear that she wanted no contact with corpses, and in any case you needed a diploma to deal with them; so she would concentrate on the managerial side, which she now had taped. I could see that she was a virtuoso with the official forms involved: among these were one to release the body from the mortuary (two doctors had to sign this and charged an outrageous fee for doing so, another restrictive practice of interest to the competition lawyer) and one – possibly the same form – called The Green, which seemed to be especially important. Confident that she could compete on price and offer a service more imaginative and sympathetic than that provided by conventional undertakers, she started playing with ideas, in search of her USP. The mourners would be encouraged to decorate the coffin, as she had the Mummies': it would be on a table, around which they would sit, condoling, consoling and sharing memories. Her relationship with the bereaved would be intimate and caring. In appropriate circumstances she would arrange a 'cheerful funeral'. 'I'll transform the image of undertaking!' she proclaimed in the manner of Steve Ballmer. Soon she was on to straplines: 'Good To

Go' she liked and 'See You Later At The Cremator'.

I was sceptical. Who would want a cheerful funeral? Families who had hated the deceased, perhaps, but how many would admit to that? As to the intimate and caring bit, which seemed to merge undertaking with agony-aunting, Fluffy is wont to spend hours on the phone advising girlfriends about their emotional dramas: if she lavished the same time on the bereaved, the body would have rotted before it reached the crem. I also worried about the response of the undertakers' guild if they found their market shares eroded by snazzy packages from the bargain basement: they were, as we knew, a rough bunch and would have no trouble disposing of a competitor's corpse, or of her husband's.

Then there was the problem of finding room for the necessary kit, for Fluffy proposed to run the business from our house, which was already stuffed with the paraphernalia of her interior-design enterprise. Our front hall is a warehouse not only for fabric samples, tiles, cornice fragments, and other people's furniture, but also – she has long used the intimate and caring approach in this domain – for her clients' laundry, repaired shoes, ironing boards and mail deliveries. The coffins, she declared, would be kept in the loft. I didn't like the sound of that, for access to our loft is via a trapdoor in the ceiling of my study: a traffic of coffins would disturb my concentration, chip my bibelots, and irritate Maud, who likes to sleep on a chair in the corner. We would also, Fluffy asserted, need two large freezers, which would have to go in the back yard. Again I had concerns, for I was thinking of keeping a pig there: the freezers would reduce the animal's *Lebensraum*, and a pig might, if given the chance, try to eat the corpses. Fluffy waved these objections away on the ground that it was impossible for us to have a pig: the yard was paved, and pigs needed soft soil in order to root for truffles. I replied that there were no truffles in the soil of Tower Hamlets, and Fluffy retorted that this proved her point. 'A pair of king-size freezers would be just the job,' she went on, now trying to cajole me. 'We'll also be able to use them for chops and things.' I played the Health and Safety card and pointed to the hideous mix-ups that could result if her business required her to store detached body-parts: we could find ourselves eating one of her customers in a fry-up. The only advantage of these freezers, so far as I could see, was that they provided a convenient means of suicide, which I sometimes contemplated. If I froze myself to death in one of them, the initial steps would already have been completed when Fluffy took me over in her professional capacity.

She discovered that hearses, like coffins, are available at reasonable prices on eBay. Ours, she said, would go in our parking space in the private road behind the house. Our right to the space is disputed by the woman next door, and I suggested that the dispute might escalate if a twenty-foot hearse replaced our Jazz. Talking over me, Fluffy went on to explain that we would need another vehicle for such non-ceremonial purposes as the collection of bodies from mortuaries: a Ford Galaxy, with blackened windows, was the standard issue. This, apparently, was to be kept in front of the house, in our other parking space, so I could not work out where the Jazz was to go. 'And since we live in the East End,' Fluffy said, warming to the theme, 'we should think about horses. Gangland loves a horse-drawn hearse. They used one for Jack the Hat McVitie.' I was sure that Jack the Hat had been dumped in the sea (or was it the lake in Vicky Park?) by Brown Bread Fred, but I directed my fire on practical issues. Where would the horses be kept? In the back yard? Who would muck them out? What would the pig make of them? Fluffy reminded me that we were not getting a pig, and accused me of being a nay-sayer.

It didn't happen. My wife, like Mr Toad, is prone to crazes which peter out (her version is that, like Leonardo da Vinci, she has more ideas than time to develop them), and the funeral project was soon replaced by a wheeze for selling smoothies through the front window, and this in turn by one for transporting fabrics across the Sahara by camel. She would incorporate the fabrics in her designs for interiors, she said, so there would be synergies.

The Fluffy Diet

For a while, my wife Fluffy was keen on making fairy cakes. It was a blissful period in our marriage. We each ate at least ten per day. Metabolically blessed, I remained the same shape and weight, but Fluffy started to expand into a walrus, her weight exceeding mine for the first time. (Since then, the graph lines of our weights have twined around each other.) Realising that something had to be done, she substituted for the fairy cakes a diet of raw vegetables, which she told me would ward off cancer. Not one to do things by halves, she swings between Trimalchionian excess and stylitic mortification, and, since she prepares most of our meals, I'm pulled along in her wake. I strongly prefer the excessive phases, but I agreed to have a go with the raw vegetables, some of which she ground to a brown pulp in an antique machine that was going cheap on eBay. When I drew the line at celery for breakfast, she allowed me a specially penitential muesli, like gravel, with low-fat soya milk. Although binge eating doesn't make me fatter, ascetic dieting does make me thinner; as my cheeks began to hollow, and my neck to withdraw from my collars, friends expressed concern. One asked whether I had cancer.

Shortly after I dipped below nine stone, and Fluffy below ten, her willpower gave out, and we swung to steaks, sausages, trifle and banoffee pie. Then she read that you live longer if you eat very small portions. Apparently scientists had established this with mice – but then mice eat very small portions in the ordinary course, and their lives are short. There ensued a few weeks in which I had to hunt on the plate for my dinner: the ratio of plate to food was *nouvelle cuisine*, but our plates are much smaller than those in NC restaurants. I played along at mealtimes, but kept a chicken-and-ham pie in my study.

Fluffy next decided to be a vegan, for reasons of her own health and the welfare of dumb creatures. She joined the Vegan Society, which has a stock of films showing the dreadful things done to animals for the sake of our carniverous habit. To buttress her resolve, she asked the Society to send her the most shocking films, which she invited me to watch with her on DVD. I declined, and settled down to read, but concentration was shattered by her howls and sobs. At the end she started to tell me what she had seen. 'I don't want to know,' I shouted, and put my fingers in my ears, but as soon as I had pulled them out she carried on telling me. In the worst scene, a pig in a slaughterhouse was hoisted high into the air in a sling which, not being properly fastened, dropped the animal, breaking all its legs under its own great weight.

Outraged and fervid, Fluffy went to a meeting of the Society at Conway Hall.[1] The other people attending were weird, smelly and sickly. Alienated, disheartened, and oppressed by a longing for a juicy pork chop, Fluffy started eating meat again. When she does so, she can't banish the films from her mind, and so our Sunday lunches are broken by more howling.

In the matter of dietary fads, Fluffy rivals my friend Hamish, who sprinkles on his meals a powder which carries out part of the digestive process before he puts the food in his mouth. I offered to serve him a turd on a plate to make things still easier. Hamish swears by Japanese seaweed, which he both eats and puts in the bath, and he reveres Dr C Orian Truss, creator of the mucus-free diet; I don't remember whether it is a diet that contains no mucus or one that eliminates it from the eater. Hamish is also a fan of Maximilian Bircher-Benner, the inventor of muesli. On his wall he has a frame containing two faded photos, one of B-B and another of his own grandfather, the engineer of the Tay Bridge, who looked rather similar to the muesli man.

In order to eat vegetables too exotic for the local greengrocer, Hamish rented an allotment. When he took it over, it was a wilderness of weeds, so the

---

[1] I have been there for a concert. It's a grim place, the rooms of which are named after figures revered by the Ethical Society, such as Bertrand Russell and William Johnson Fox. An 'Events Today' sign announced that the anti-hunting meeting would take place in the Fox Room.

tenant of the neighbouring patch offered him a flamethrower that would clear them in a jiffy. Like a hose, the device had a nozzle that could be adjusted for a spray or a thin jet. When Hamish set it for the thinnest of jets, and turned it on, it cast a shaft of flame on to the next allotment but one, incinerating a marrow. The allotment committee evicted him before his first Chinese long bean poked out a stalk.

London's Leading
Hypochondriac

Psychiatrists, who like to invent illnesses, have come up with GAD, short for Generalised Anxiety Disorder, which means that you worry a lot. I am a textbook case. The anxiety is constant in level but variable in topic. Some years ago I was gripped by worry about a terrorist attack in London. Life was going well: I was earning plenty of money as a lawyer, I was finishing a book, and I was engaged to Fluffy, with whom I was sharing a flat in the Barbican. One morning the thought struck me that the office block across the road would be a good place for a jihadist to plant a bomb. A ramp led down to a space under the block, for deliveries. I stared out of the window, watching the vans go down the ramp and wondering which one contained the bomb that would kill or maim Fluffy and me.

The anxiety grew so intense that I proposed our

moving to the country. Knowing nothing of rural life, Fluffy liked the idea, so we started contemplating safe retreats. I ruled out Suffolk and Norfolk on the ground that, since the prevailing wind in Britain is south-westerly, any radiation from a dirty bomb in London would drift over East Anglia. Fluffy fancied Yorkshire, having once spent a blissful weekend there with a former fiancé. In my eyes that was not an attraction; I also had bad memories of a week-long walking tour of the dales in 1967.[1] To dissuade Fluffy from that county, I laid its cons on thick. Although I could do some work from home, I would need to be in London at least

---

[1] The trip, organised by the Youth Hostels Association, was advertised for boys aged ten to fifteen. My school friend Robby and I were ten, but the other boys in the group, working-class lads from Huddersfield (which they called Oodders), were at the upper end of the range. They found a pair of Fauntleroys from South Kensington hilarious, and roared at our pronunciation, but once the mockery had run its course we got on well, and they found Robby and me useful as criminal accomplices. A gaggle of us would enter a tobacconist and, while we two engaged the shopkeeper in genteel conversation, our rough friends would nick packets of fags. They also urged us to distract a vicar while they broke open a church collection box, but we drew the line at that. The tour was led by a weedy young man called Neil – we rechristened him Nelly – who got us lost on the first day; this was meant to comprise a gentle introductory stroll of five miles, but we ended up walking a zigzag route of twenty miles through fog over a moor. My boots were the old-fashioned kind that needed breaking in and, although I had stomped around our flat in them for the week before the trip, they were still so stiff that Nelly's detour scraped most of the skin from my heels and toes. The rest of the week was misery. As I hobbled over more moor the next day, I fought back tears when I saw a train speeding towards London. We trudged towards a ventilator shaft over the tunnel into which the train had disappeared; here the Oodders boys waited until another train entered the tunnel, and then they dropped rocks down the shaft.

three days a week, so for much of the time she would be alone in the middle of nowhere. In the winter it would be dark at four; there would be at least another seven hours until bedtime, the wind would be howling, and the rain beating against the windows. The washing would freeze on the line; trousers would stand up by themselves when she unpegged them. I overdid it, and she went off country life altogether, refusing to budge from the terrorists' bull's-eye.

After a few weeks, I got bored with worrying about bombs, and my GAD moved on to the mercury fillings in my teeth, which I decided were giving me brain damage. As I searched for signs, it seemed to me that I was forgetting more and more, that my speech was slurring, that my movements were jerky and uncoordinated. Why had no one said anything? Terror-stricken, I made an appointment with my dentist, Mr Nuttall, to discuss replacing the fillings with non-metallic ones. My view of Nuttall was dim, but inertia caused me to stick with him. On one occasion he started drilling on the wrong side of my mouth; when I squawked, his apology was perfunctory. On another, when I arrived for an appointment, his receptionist turned me away on the ground that he was dealing with an emergency; through the door to the surgery I could hear giggles and squeals of a sexual nature, and his nurse Angie then emerged, flushed and adjusting her bra.[2]

---

[2] Perhaps dentists generally are highly sexed. When I was younger and more attractive, I visited one who, having tipped me back in the chair, rested her hand on my thigh and gazed hungrily into my eyes. At the

Nuttall had a more businesslike relationship with Angie's successor, Doreen, an introverted person with a permanent cold. 'Ace amalgam, Dor,' he would say to jolly her along. 'Ace amalgam' was one of his stock phrases, others being 'I'm going to palpate your jaw' and 'We can brighten up that smile.' Regular patients who knew each other would play Nuttall Bingo: you got a point for each slogan he uttered during your visit. Like many dentists, he kept Classic FM on in the background, to soothe the patient. *A Night on the Bare Mountain* was playing while he gave me root-canal work.

Nuttall asserted that mercury fillings were perfectly safe, and then, with doubtful consistency, that it was riskier to drill them out than to leave them in: they were like asbestos in buildings. I was not comforted, but my anxiety was already hunting for a new topic, which it found in the fact that my firm was laying people off: I would be sacked, unable to find another job, destitute and homeless. As always, the problem was not the topic but the anxiety itself; recognising that the former is just a temporary hook on which to hang the latter can be some relief – a second-order calm. There are only so many things you can worry about: after a while you reprise previous themes, with variations. I am now back on terrorism, this time in the form of a chemical attack on the Bank of England – an event for which, I am told, the security forces plan. The

end of the session, she told me that several more would be needed. The process was repeated three times before I caught on and changed dentists.

fumes will blow over our house in Spitalfields, making it uninhabitable and worthless, for insurers will not cover such events. I am not bothered this time about being injured or killed, but I have said to Fluffy that we should move to a small flat in West London, to protect and spread our assets. Having heard it all before, she has told me to get a grip. If I'm worried about losing money, she says, I should place a bet with William Hill – 500 to one on an unconventional attack in London during the next ten years, or something. But how do you place such a bet? Would a bookie accept it? How should it be worded? Are betting agreements enforceable?

My favourite topic is my health. A friend recently introduced me as London's leading hypochondriac. This word has shifted in meaning over the years, and nowadays is used in various ways that are often elided. It is applied, or misapplied, to someone who (1) is not ill but believes he is; or (2) takes his minor ailments for major ones; or (3) worries unduly about his health; or (4) is not ill, or seriously ill, but pretends to be; or (5) has an illness with a mental cause; or (6) has symptoms that doctors can't explain. The distinctions ramify. As to (1), presumably the belief must be unreasonable, but how unreasonable must it be? As to (3), where is the boundary between undue worry and prudent concern? As to all the above, what is an illness? Are you ill if you feel ill, or only if your body malfunctions? What is it to feel ill? I could go on.

I fall into all six categories, especially (3) – for

which 'valetudinarian' is a more accurate word than 'hypochondriac'. By the bed I keep a medical encyclopedia. Often, when I am looking up a condition I think I may have, my eye is caught by an entry for some other one beginning with the same letter, and I start worrying about that. By this process I have moved from 'cold' to 'cholera', and from 'rash' to 'rabies'. A valetudinarian can always find something on which to hook his anxiety – a tender gland in the neck (sign of mumps), a mild rash (shingles), a dry throat (Ebola), a lack of energy (almost anything) – but I am an odd case in that the anxiety does not depend on my identifying a serious illness: whereas your standard valetudinarian will cry 'I've got a dry throat – oh Jesus, it must be *Ebola*,' I will cry 'Oh Jesus, I've got a *dry throat!*' and wring my hands in torment. It's ridiculous and contemptible, of course, but knowing that makes no difference.

I attribute my dread of illness to a spell in hospital at the age of two. My mother, thinking I looked peaky, decided that the best remedy was an outing to the park in my pushchair. It was an icy day. On our return, I fell asleep in my highchair over supper. Alarmed, she took my temperature and found that it was 105 degrees. The doctor was summoned, pronounced that I had pneumonia, and rang for an ambulance. I stayed in hospital ten days, and was so poorly that I was put in a room by myself with a steam kettle. In that era, visiting hours were severely limited; my mother was not allowed to stay with me on the night of my admission, and the following morning, when she arrived at the hospital, we gazed desperately at each other from passing lifts, as she went up to the children's ward and I went down for an X-ray. On each of the ten days, she brought me Fuzzy-Felts or other toys to cheer me up, but at the end of visiting time I would wail with grief and demand that all toys be removed from the bed. Illness was thus, for me, welded to loss, isolation and terror.

It is unfortunate if, like Vera, my GP and friend, you are both a valetudinarian and a doctor, for then you have a wider repertoire of concern. For the layman, there is the standing threat of germs. Not long after the pneumonia incident, my mother explained to me the importance of washing my hands after going to the lavatory. From then I would carry on like Lady Macbeth. When, at the end of an ablution, I accidentally touched the lav seat, I flew into a frenzy: 'Now I'm covered in GERMS!' This fear persisted into adulthood. At the office, in order to avoid germs, I would push doors open with my elbow, wash my hands in the least convenient, and hence the least fingered, basin in the gents, breathe out hard when passing anyone who was coughing, and use the phone to talk to a colleague with a cold, even if he was in the next room. If Fluffy and I went to the theatre, and I found myself next to a cold-sufferer, I would contrive to change places with Fluffy – offering to swap so as to give her a better view or, if the sizes of the people in front of us made the offer absurd, leaping into her seat after the interval. She soon realised what was going on, and has since volunteered to be coughed upon, in order to avoid the charade. When she herself has a cold, I will embrace her only from behind, my head averted. Oddly, when our cat Maud sneezes in my face, I'm worried not for myself but for Maud – a case of vicarious valetudinarianism. Nor do I mind when I *get* a cold: it's the anticipation, not the condition, that is so upsetting. I read that Londoners felt the same about the Blitz.

When I was nine, I became convinced that my left leg was becoming longer than my right, and that soon I would have to wear a surgical boot. To compare the lengths of the legs, I would kneel with my feet against the wall and see which knee stuck out further; a bit of shuffling ensured that the left one always did. I started walking with a limp. Uncle Jack tried to get me to laugh it off: 'Don't worry,' he said; 'if your left leg is longer, the right one is shorter by exactly the same amount, to compensate.' I was not amused. Shortly afterwards, when my mother was turning up a pair of trousers for me, she pointed out that my right leg was half an inch longer than my left. I adjusted my anxiety, and my limp, accordingly. Then I heard a friend of my mother's mention that you could tell a lunatic by the fact that, when he walks, he swings his right arm with his right leg, and his left arm with his left leg, rather than swinging diagonally, as it were. I had never given thought to the way my arms swung, but, with a bit of practice, managed to convince myself that I was a lunatic.

Once I had wearied of my legs and arms, I started to worry that I was deaf in my left ear. My parents had been concerned about my hearing when I was a toddler and still too young to think about my own health (golden days). Their GP advised them to carry out a makeshift test at home, so my father played a game with me in which we knelt on opposite sides of a door and whispered to each other through the keyhole. He couldn't hear me, but I could hear him perfectly well. They put my deafness down to disobedience. My own anxiety about my hearing had some basis in fact, for I had suffered from bad adenoids which had given me blocked ears. They (the adenoids) were removed at the Throat, Nose and Ear Hospital, a Victorian relic off Regent Street. There being no room in the children's ward, I was dismayed to be put in with the grown men next door; but the men were infantile and friendly, they admired my koala bear, they had 'borrowed' the children's Lego, and they enjoyed watching children's telly – their favourite being *Champion the Wonder Horse*, to the theme tune of which they sang along. The operation was performed by Mr Alan Rotter, who had extracted my mother's tonsils. It was my mother's second tonsillectomy, the first having taken place, when she was a girl, on the kitchen table; in those days, tonsils were chopped off rather than uprooted, and hers grew again. She told me that she had not felt frightened until the surgeon – it may have been the barber – had said 'Don't be frightened.' Perhaps I inherited my nervous disposition from her. To cheer her up after the second op, my father brought to the hospital a half-bottle of champagne for them to drink together. The bubbles caused her agony.

A Rotter's work on my adenoids unblocked my ears, but it seemed to me that the left one was no longer as good as the right. I would compare them, as I had compared my legs – putting my finger first over one ear, then over the other, cocking my head, straining to hear faint sounds, and attracting puzzled looks from passers-by. In the decades since, this topic has come round every so often. Recently, when I noticed that, if I lay in bed on my right side, I could not hear the rain on the roof, I was so worried that I made an appointment with a specialist at Cromwell Hospital. 'That's where George Best had his liver swap,' Fluffy said, and I momentarily wondered who in their right mind would swap livers with George. Before seeing the consultant, I was given a hearing test by a Middle Eastern woman wearing a scarf, which may have impaired *her* hearing. The test was conducted in a room by a staircase up and down which people kept thundering, and in the next room a party or an argument was in full swing: it was hard to discern the noises in my headphones from others in the rumpus, so I was not reassured when the consultant told me that my hearing was fine. Instead, I booked a free test at Amplifon, the hearing-aid shop in Wigmore Street: since they had an interest in finding something wrong with me, I could rely on them not to gloss over horrifying facts.

It is embarrassing to be seen entering a hearing-aid shop, so I sidled in. I can recommend the place if you want to get out of the rain and spend a peaceful hour before a Wigmore Hall concert: it's warm, the people are nice, and they give you a cup of tea. The woman who conducted the test knew her onions, and there were no noises off. At the end she said 'You don't hear as well in your left ear as you do in your right' – I broke into a sweat, I *knew* there was something wrong – 'but that's because the hearing in your right ear is exceptionally good' – I whimpered with relief and wanted to hug her – 'for someone of your age.' Of my age? What was I to make of that? If most fifty-eight-year-olds can't hear the rain, hearing aids should be mandatory at fifty-five, and Amplifon would be raking it in.

The deafness of others is funny, if you are cruel or unimaginative enough. Mr Grummett, one of the masters at my public school, had an old-fashioned hearing aid, with a wire running into a box in his pocket. Sometimes, when he entered the classroom, we would all speak very quietly, he would turn the volume up, and then one of us would ask him a question in a booming voice, making him jump. Poor Grummett also suffered from ringing in the ears, as I have ever since the adenoid days. In my case it's usually a high G sharp, somewhere between the ears, and certain real noises, such as that of a taxi motor, reverberate in my head. The trouble comes and goes, and is most noticeable when I am ill, tired or anxious; the tinnitus itself causing anxiety, there is a vicious spiral. Bad attacks are triggered by horror stories such as that of the policeman whose noise was so oppressive that he jumped off Beachy Head. This was told to me by the President of the Totteridge and Whetstone Tinnitus Society, who claimed to have been elected because his ears rang the loudest.

My noisiest period was when I was unhappily engaged, to a predecessor of Fluffy's. When we became disengaged, the ringing stopped immediately, but before that I became so distressed that I consulted Vera, who sent me for an MRI scan in the crypt of a deconsecrated church. I lay on a sliding shelf and was pushed into the mouth of what looked like a giant washing machine. 'Make sure you don't move your head,' the technician said through the headphones she had put on me, whereupon I felt an urge to nod and shake it. The scan took about half an hour, the machine sounding like a choir of pneumatic drills, which drowned the tinnitus. 'If you feel claustrophobic,' she said, 'give us a shout and we'll pull you out'; but, apart from the effort not to wobble my head, it was a strangely soothing experience. To pacify nervous patients, someone had stuck a few gold stars, like those from a schoolbook, on the ceiling of the tunnel in which I lay. A week later I visited Dr Diggory, the consultant in charge of the MRI, to learn the results, and he handed me a couple of photos showing cross-sections of my head. 'Nothing wrong with you,' Diggory said. 'No tumours or anything like that. Brain's completely normal.' (He shunned the definite article; perhaps he had Russian ancestry.) Then he smiled condescendingly and got up, we shook hands, and I left the room, too cowed to remind him that my problem was not my brain but my tinnitus, which he had not cured, explained, or even mentioned. The bill was over £1,000.

I was allowed to keep the pictures, which I

examined on the way home. My cheeks looked grotesquely plump, like those of a baby. Perhaps these cheeks *were* a baby's, and Diggory had muddled up his patients. Perhaps the right photos showed a monstrous tumour pressing on the nerves from my ears. Such mix-ups happen. When a novel of mine was published, Fluffy arranged a launch party, for which she ordered a cake in the form of the book, the cover reproduced in icing sugar. Vera took some snaps of it on her mobile phone and told me she would send them by email. No cake was visible in the pictures I received, which seemed to be of some lamb cutlets. A minute later I got another message from Vera, urgently asking me to delete the preceding one, and explaining that she had absentmindedly attached some X-rays of a patient's spinal column. I wondered whether she had sent the pictures of my cake to the patient, who would have been even more startled to see 'A novel by Oliver Black' inscribed on his spine.

Even when a medical picture is of the right thing, it can be of poor quality. When I had a persistent cough, Vera sent me for an X-ray, which showed a shadow on my right lung. 'I'm sure it's nothing,' she said over-brightly, 'but I'll refer you to a lung man, just to check.' The lung man told me I would need an MRI. 'Should I be worried?' I asked. 'We'll discuss life expectancy next time,' he replied. It was a joke, but he had misjudged his audience. I was so agitated that, when trying to leave, I walked into a cupboard and fell over a broom. The MRI revealed that the shadow had been caused by my not standing close enough to the X-ray machine. 'Thank heavens – I was *so* worried!' Vera unprofessionally exclaimed, adding the lung man's report to my bulging file. I knew for the future what she meant by 'I'm sure it's nothing'.

To my insurance company's chagrin, I have had MRI scans for many other complaints, including mild dizziness. I was especially alarmed by this, for it had been the first symptom of the brain tumour that killed my father. As usual, I monitored myself constantly, shutting my eyes and trying either to walk a straight line or to stand on one leg. The cat was frightened by my swaying around.

For the tinnitus, I have tried various remedies, none of them successful. A colleague recommended bananas, on the ground that they contained magnesium, but he could not explain why that was relevant. For a couple of weeks I stuffed myself with four a day. The only result was constipation. Fluffy pooh-poohed the idea that bananas have a binding effect, but it is confirmed by Beckett in *Krapp's Last Tape*. She suggested that I try what she called 'aquapuncture', so I made an appointment with a Chinese practitioner called Mabel Ma, whose practice was in a terraced house in Mile End. Mabel led me into the front room, where she told me to take off my shoes and socks and lie on the table, which had a hole in it. 'Ress yo hea' in thee ho,' she said, and then stuck a cluster of needles behind each of my ears, and a few more in my arms, hands and feet. Don't believe anyone who says that acupuncture is painless: Mabel pushed each needle in till I yelped. Some she heated to a scorching temperature. Once they were all in, she told me that she would come back in twenty minutes. Lying there, a supine porcupine, I became drowsy, but was jolted into alertness by a pattering sound on the floor. I didn't dare move to investigate the cause, in case any needles fell out or went further in, but took it to be the sausage dog which had been sleeping in the hall when I arrived. I was now waiting for it to leap on to my stomach – unlikely, given the respective lengths of its legs and the table's.

On my second visit, Mabel produced a small box from which there hung wires with clips at the ends. She attached each clip to one of the needles behind my ears, plugged the box into the mains, and pressed a button which sent a current into the needles. My face started twitching and, as Mabel turned a dial on the front of the box, the twitches blossomed into kaleidoscopic grimaces. Again she left me there, in full view of the pedestrians just outside the window, which gave directly on to the pavement. What if someone I knew looked in? Did I know anyone in Mile End? Acupuncturists should take more care to provide a comfortable environment. I later visited one who practised in a building behind the London Coliseum; in the basement was a hall which English National Opera used for rehearsals. As the needles went in, there was a burst of the Anvil Chorus.

Acupuncture has effects – after each session I would feel tired and weepy – but the cure of tinnitus is not among them. Admitting defeat, Mabel referred me to a Dr Ding, whose surgery was in a Soho basement. The cramped waiting area there was packed: a third of the patients were Chinese, two

thirds English, and of these one half were desperate –
Western medicine having washed its hands of them –
and the other mad. The woman squashed next to me
on the bench tried to start a conversation. 'When I
left home this morning,' she said, 'my husband was
just eighteen inches tall.' That was a modest height, I
replied. 'You should see my son,' she went on: 'he's
got *lovely* pubic hair.' I smiled distantly and
pretended to read my *TLS*.

Ding's consulting room was not a room – rather,
a cubicle separated from the waiting area by some
hardboard which, as in a public lavatory, was nailed to
posts and reached to neither the floor nor the ceiling.
Consultations were thus audible to those on the other
side. When it was my turn, I whispered why I had
come, averting my eyes from the posters, sellotaped to
the hardboard, of the loathsome skin-conditions that
were Ding's speciality. She said almost nothing in
reply, and our meeting lasted less than two minutes,
at the end of which she wrote a prescription in
logograms and told me to take it to the pharmacist
next door. There I inspected jars of twigs, and of
unidentified extracts from animals of endangered
species, before being handed a bottle containing pills
so large that a horse would have had trouble with
them. 'Take ten, four times a day,' said the label.
The idea may have been that the rattling of the pills
in my tummy would distract me from the ringing in
my ears. Apart from wasting my time and straining
my gullet, the pills had no detectable effect, but they
may have done undetectable damage – Chinese
medicine differing from, say, homeopathy in using

strong drugs. When a friend of mine applied a Chinese cream for hives, all her hair fell out.

My eyesight has given me as much gyp as my hearing. One of my childhood anxieties was about seeing double: if I looked at a bright line against a dark background, the line would duplicate or blur. I was not imagining it, but the ophthalmologist could find nothing wrong, and I then forgot about it for some years; but when I was in my twenties I mentioned the problem to a girlfriend whose father was a luminary at Moorfields, and she arranged a backdoor appointment at his clinic. The session I attended was for toddlers, who, apart from a blind one, were running around the waiting room and yelling. When the nurse took me for a test of vision, I was made to sit in a tiny chair, and the test, being for those of less than reading age, used pictures instead of letters. Nurse, unable to adjust her manner, addressed me in a *Listen With Mother* voice: 'Now then, gorgeous, tell me if the little red sheep is brighter than the big green cow.' I answered with dignity. Again they could find nothing wrong. The consultant, my squeeze's father, severely said 'Your eyes are OK – it must be in your brain.' It was unclear whether he meant that I was making it up, which was insulting, or that I had a brain disorder, which was frightening.

I have been to Moorfields twice since. The next time was when I noticed that, as I read down a page, the print would change in size. Again the doctor was nonplussed: 'It's a visual phenomenon,' he announced, which I would have thought was obvious

– but perhaps 'visual', as used in those circles, is a term of art. Does it mean the same as 'in your brain'? To examine my retinas, this man put in some drops to dilate my pupils; when I left the hospital, I was so dazzled by the sunlight that I had almost to close my eyes and felt my way along the railings by the pavement. I left Moorfields blinder than I had gone in.

The other time was late one Sunday evening when I noticed a large floater in my right eye and decided that it was a detached retina. I had read that these need prompt attention, and so, leaving Fluffy to eat by herself the roast dinner she had spent the last two hours preparing, I dashed off to outpatients, where I was told to wait until the triage nurse could take my details. She was busy behind a curtain with another patient, whom I could hear spelling out letters in a foreign accent: M B O B I L W E. An African giving his name, I assumed. When it was my turn, the nurse gave me a vision test. First I had to read some letters on a screen: M B O B I – after that, they were too small. Next she asked me to look at two shapes, one on a red background, the other on a green one – the counterparts of the little red sheep and the big green cow of yore. 'Which of these two circles is more round?' she asked. I was too anxious to give a pedantic reply. In any case, you might defend the question on the ground that 'perfect' adds something to 'circle'.

The next outpatients department I visited was at the Hospital for Tropical Diseases. One morning, just before setting off for work, I was wiping my bottom and thought I felt something wriggling in the paper. I ignored it, but, when I glanced into the bowl, I saw a large worm writhing among the turds and paper. I had no time to do anything about it, for I had a meeting at the office, so I ordered Fluffy not to go into the downstairs lav, and certainly not to flush it: I would explain later. The meeting, a stressful one, prompted another motion, and I was terrified of expelling a Medusan tangle of giant worms. I could feel them in my abdomen. When I entered the gents, one of the two cubicles was occupied. As I sat in the other, I gave a small scream as the turd started to emerge. There were no worms, and in my relief I forgot to sit tight until my neighbour had gone. It was my boss, who left his cubicle just as I left mine. We tacitly agreed to forget the scream.

I scuttled to my office, dreamt up an urgent errand for my trainee, shut the door, and phoned Vera, who, admitting that she had never come across such a thing, told me to take the worm to the Hospital for Tropical Diseases. When I got home, I raided the kitchen for a slotted spoon, a pair of chopsticks and a tupperware box, took a deep breath and entered the lav. The creature was floating shrivelled and motionless, but, as soon as I reached into the bowl with the chopsticks, it burst into vigorous life, and I had to chase it around the turds. Coaxing it into the box was the very devil, and when I succeeded it refused to calm down. I wondered whether I should offer it something to eat, and, if so, what.

At the hospital I saw a doctor who was being shadowed by a student – the latter a beefy and sportsmanlike young man. When I opened the box, the worm, which had been having a nap, started prancing about again. The student screamed, more loudly, and for longer, than I had done at the office. He would, I reflected, need to toughen up if he was to have a career treating beriberi, jiggers and yaws. (Why do ghastly diseases have cheery names?) The doctor, having peered more closely at the worm than I had dared to, asked me whether our lavatory was on the ground floor. Yes, I replied. 'I thought so,' she said: 'it's a common earthworm – they often get into downstairs loos. I'll send it upstairs, to confirm.' So I had imagined the wriggling in the paper, and the worm's visit at the time had been a coincidence. The student, breathing heavily, was dispatched upstairs, with the worm in its box. 'They won't hurt it?' I nearly asked; the threat having dwindled, I was becoming fond of the animal. The box was empty when it was returned with the confirmation, my invertebrate pal having been suspended in formaldehyde or worse.

My law firm provided health checks to its employees, the checks' frequency increasing with the employee's age. Once you had hit forty, you had one every other year, and Dr Goldie, who conducted them, would start dropping the phrase 'at your age' into the conversation (cf. the Amplifon lady). In a variant locution he told me that I was moving from the age of testicular cancer to the age of prostate cancer, which I decided was good news, having recently consulted Vera about an aching testicle. Vera looked uncomfortable as she explored my scrotum – we have always been on platonic terms – and I was mildly offended by her donning plastic gloves for the exercise. The groping over, she walked to the other end of the room to, as she put it, see how my testicles were hung – as if they were weights of an antique clock.

A session with Dr Goldie comprised various tests. The one for prostate cancer used to be an iatric finger in the anus – which I always found pleasurable, especially when the finger, covered with gel, was smoothly withdrawn – but later it was done with a blood sample. The bloodletting was useful, but some of the other tests were silly. Goldie ordered me to touch my toes, which I couldn't do – but so what? Then he produced a pair of metal bars, about six inches long, which were attached to each other by a sprung hinge at the bottom. This was to measure the strength of my grip. 'Take the bars in one hand,' he said, 'and, when I tell you, press them as close together as you can. One, two, three, *go!*' I squeezed with all my might, my face went red, and the veins bulged on my temples, but I couldn't move the bars. 'Well go on, then,' Goldie said impatiently, thinking that I hadn't started. When I received his written report, it said 'Exceptionally weak grip' – but again it was not clear why that mattered. I could pick up cutlery and pens (now, when I did so, I congratulated myself), I could manage self-abuse, and legal work didn't require a vice-like grip. Perhaps clients liked a firm handshake. Then there was the questionnaire to determine whether you were depressed. The questions were obscurely worded – for example 'On a scale of one to ten, how happy are you?' It all depended on how you understood the numbers. Was one a state of indifference or of suicidal misery? I was chugging along at the time, but not especially joyful, so I hazarded four. Goldie's report stated that I should be monitored as a borderline depressive.

These reports, in the form of a letter to me, always concluded 'Overall, you are in excellent health' – a message that suited my employers, who paid for the examination – but as I moved into my fifties, and the checks' frequency increased to one a year, the conclusion decreased in plausibility. I suffered an assortment of physical symptoms, I had alarming feelings of dread and unreality, and I spent more and more time wiped out in bed. Vera, who stated in body language that I was a hypochondriac (in one or more of the senses listed above), sent me to a 'specialist general physician', who put my symptoms down to overwork, a diagnosis I had already reached by myself. Fluffy, who had to put up with my moaning and shuffling around the house in a nightie, thought that the doctors were fobbing me off. Deaf to my protests, she went on the internet in search of alternative remedies.

Her first catch was SEC, The Systemic Examination Centre, an outfit in Belgravia which offered a full review and analysis of ailments that had resisted diagnosis elsewhere. It turned out to be a double act performed by two retired Italian doctors,

Professor Pazzi and Doctor Zulli. Pazzi was bearded, fat, expensively dressed and highly perfumed, and spoke English in archaic RP; Zulli was glabrous, wiry, shabby, and musty in smell, and had the stock accent. 'You av pain in stomacha,' he told me as he felt that area. 'No I don't,' I replied. He pressed his thumb hard under my navel, and I winced. '*Now* you av pain in stomacha,' he said, smiling with his mouth only. Diagnosis was by an exchange between the two men, in front of the patient: Zulli would make a timid suggestion, Pazzi would ridicule it and propose a hypothesis of his own, to which Zulli would humbly propose refinements. 'Mmm, it could be Wilson's disease,' Pazzi mused, wiggling a beringed finger, and sent me for some blood tests. I was in torment while I waited for the results, my encyclopedia having told me that Wilson's disease, a rare condition caused by an accumulation of copper, can lead to insanity and death. One night I had a coded dream of having the disease: I was in Swindon with the Elizabethan composer John Cooper. What has that got to do with it? Well, I once stayed in Swindon with a family called Wilson, and John Cooper had Italianised his name to Coperario: copper, rare, io – I, in the Italian spoken by my doctors. Freud was on to something.

Pazzi announced that the results were negative, which, in my panic, I took to mean that I had the disease. He sorted out negative and positive for me. Then the dialectic recommenced, issuing in another hair-raising hypothesis, which had to be tested in turn. As well as having blood tests, I had to collect twenty-four hours' worth of urine in a large plastic pot, which a motorcyclist came to collect from our house; he slid it into a pannier, and the sloshing of the liquid caused him to wobble as he drove off. After some weeks of this, I was drained of bodily fluids and traumatised by suspense, and told Fluffy that I would not see the Italians again. She put up a fight, ostensibly on medical grounds, but I knew that she enjoyed the consultations, to which she insisted on accompanying me. She fancied Pazzi, who would bow and kiss her hand on each occasion; I could smell his cologne on it afterwards. It was a dangerous situation: I was a burnt-out wreck, and he was a successful, handsome and vigorous man. 'I'm never sick,' he tactlessly boasted as she gazed into his eyes. 'I don't know what illness is!' A startling declaration from a doctor. 'I hope you get Wilson's disease,' I thought. The following week he caught pneumonia, and had to cancel our meeting.

Fluffy now decided that I must be eating the wrong things, so she made an appointment for me to see a Dr Kluth, whose website boasted that he could cure the most baffling conditions by diet. Based in Stuttgart, he was on a visit to London and offering consultations at the Mermaid Clinic, a temple of alternative therapy in Tooting. Kluth was in such demand that the only time he could offer was seven a.m. Before seeing him I was to fast for twelve hours. The first I heard of any of this was at six-fifty the preceding evening, when Fluffy told me that I would have to go without supper and get up before sunrise. My answer was dusty, but she is hard to gainsay.

She again insisted on coming into the consulting

room, where Kluth, a swarthy and choleric man, sat behind a desk on which there was nothing but a small pad of graph paper, one neat row of crayons in many colours, and another of Post-its, ditto. Beside him was a fey young thing called Siggy. Kluth ordered Siggy to hand me a questionnaire, which Siggy, with a sudden wild grin, whipped from a drawer and slid over the desk towards me. I leant over to fill it in. 'Nicht hier – not here!' shouted Kluth. 'Inviting room!' This seemed to mean 'in the waiting room'. He gave an impatient wave, and Siggy hustled us from the presence.

The document asked me to list everything I had eaten and drunk in the previous week. Of course I couldn't remember, so I made up half the items, and I passed over the whole packet of chocolate Hobnobs that I had abstractedly consumed in one go while watching telly. I then returned to the consulting room, Fluffy still dogging my steps, and tapped on the door. It opened nine inches, and Siggy's head appeared, surprisingly low, as if he were kneeling on the floor. I reined in my imagination. A white and podgy hand, presumably also Siggy's, then appeared and snatched my answers, and the door slammed shut.

Fluffy and I slunk back to the waiting room, where we leafed through magazines on the healing power of crystals, energy-focusing pyramids for your bed, the magic of bladderwrack, and the like, and were just girding ourselves for another knock on Kluth's door when Siggy pranced in to collect us. I noticed that he was wearing Cuban heels. Kluth, without making eye contact, motioned us to sit and pushed across the desk a coloured bar-chart which had clearly been made with the crayons. It looked like a six-year-old's maths homework. The analysis was, he said, a bit technical, and so we could skip straight to the dietary instructions which he had written on a separate sheet. The inclusions and exclusions seemed random: apples and oranges in, pears and bananas out; lamb in, beef out; milk products out, except for butter; green vegetables in, except for runner beans; no alcohol. I was to stick to the regime until I saw him when he was next in London – in six months' time. The 'no alcohol' clause did for it, I told Fluffy over our late breakfast, which in my case was doubling as the previous night's dinner: a brinner, perhaps, or a dickfast.

Yoga was what I needed, she now told me. I refused to attend a class, so she arranged for an instructor to come to the house – a sullen woman called Joy, who was in her fifties. Joy arrived wearing a mac, with just a leotard underneath. She was greasy-haired but otherwise fatless, the skin sagging off her bones. I thought of Gandhi. We would need, she said, gazing censoriously at Fluffy's heaps of rubbish in the hall, a clear expanse of floor. The bedroom was the best bet, although its floor was as uneven as Snowdonia and covered with slippery rugs through which the odd nail poked. There Joy told me that I was wearing too many clothes; she was not happy till I was reduced to vest and pants. The elastic in my Y-fronts had gone, so there was a risk of scrotal overhang. Then she took me too quickly through too many exercises, leaving me confused and with a pain in my knee. Perhaps to humiliate me, she would occasionally twist herself into positions that I had been unable to imagine and would never attempt. For the finale, she crouched on the floor, like a cat about to pounce, and invited me to crouch in the same way behind her, with my hands on her buttocks. I remembered seeing in a Victorian photo, captioned 'Rats', a line of Aborigines doing the same thing; perhaps that was where Joy, an Australian, had got the idea. As we did Rats on the floor, I looked out of the window and saw, across our narrow street, a row of young people staring at us from the office opposite. They had seen Fluffy leave the house a couple of hours earlier and were drawing their own conclusions.

Dolly and Maxi

When I moved in with Fluffy, she had a mauve motor scooter, on which she offered me pillion rides. I had been scared off these as a teenager, when my schoolfriend Giles took me for a spin on his Honda 125 and, once we had reached fifty miles an hour on the Hammersmith flyover, did a look-no-hands display. I was so shaken that, when he then banked at a corner, I leant the other way and stuck my foot out, causing us to shoot off the road. Giles later rose to an ex-police 750 cc bike and, pretending to be a speed cop, would flag motorists down to lecture them. He intended to join the police – a worrying prospect, given his violent disposition. As a small boy, he would beat his younger brother in the back of the family Cresta while their father, at the wheel, jovially called 'Everybody happy?' over his shoulder. Giles ended up as an accountant.

To entice me on to the scooter, Fluffy bought me a helmet. It seemed larger than the standard issue –

or perhaps I have an undersized head: with it on, I looked like an astronaut or a Victorian diver. Reflecting that a fifty cc machine could not be very frightening, I climbed on and found that the footrests were awkwardly far back. Perhaps my legs too are abnormal. I remembered a photo I had seen of a sheep in Cairo riding pillion on a scooter; the animal, on its way to slaughter at the end of Ramadan, was looking over the driver's shoulder as they went along, and its back legs bent the wrong way for it to rest its hooves comfortably. In England it would have been arrested for riding without a helmet, like the Sikh in that test case. (And do you remember the strike by undertakers in Dhaka, during which corpses – presumably helmetless – were given pillion rides to the mortuary?) I was wrong about the fifty cc, for an engine that feeble leaves you unable to accelerate out of trouble, which often resulted from Fluffy's delight in weaving through the traffic. At a red light, we squeezed to the front of the queue, stopping in front of a lorry, the cab of which was too high for the driver to see us. When the light went green, we remained at rest – Fluffy's mind was wandering – but the lorry started and bashed us in the back.

We were living in a 'loft' in Clerkenwell. The flat was chic, but when we bought it we failed to notice the dismal council estate that stretched out behind. The main pastime of the youths on the estate was to steal scooters, on which they buzzed around the local streets. Although Fluffy draped hers with chains and locks, it was repeatedly nicked. Whenever that happened, she retrieved it by stomping on to the estate and interrogating the available youths until they broke down. It was, you might say, a brave remedy, Fluffy's only protection being a bunch of keys, which she grasped in her fist, the keys sticking between her fingers. She never had to apply it, for her manner is persuasive. Each time she found the scooter, another part – mirror, spare wheel, seat cushion – had gone, and the machine became the equivalent of a skeleton clock. On the fifth reprise, the starter button had been gouged out, so she had to push the scooter back to the flat. Having chained it to the railings outside, she went upstairs to phone the garage. By the end of the call, it had been nicked again. Fluffy now decided to keep what remained of the scooter in the private car park under our block. Access was via a residents-only lift in which there was a CCTV camera. This, on the second day of the new regime, filmed two boys taking the scooter up and driving off. The picture was grainy, and they were wearing hoodies, so they were never caught.

The local police were uninterested. 'It's kids,' they would wearily say. If children had machine-gunned a bus queue on the Clerkenwell Road, we would have been told 'It's kids.' Over the boundary, the City police took a firmer line. When Fluffy was driving me down Aldersgate Street on the way to a dinner party, a policeman flagged us down and asked us to account for ourselves. When we took off our helmets it was clear that we were a middle-aged, middle-class couple, but the man didn't want to lose face. Dredging memories of criminal procedure from law-school days, I suggested to him that he needed reasonable grounds to stop us. That went down badly. Fluffy now became rhetorical: 'Look at him!' she said, pointing at me. 'He's wearing corduroys, a Barbour and horn-rimmed spectacles. How could he be a thief?' The policeman demanded our particulars, then told Fluffy that she had to present her papers at a police station in the next twenty-four hours. We were subdued over dinner.

Fluffy gave up reporting the thefts to the police, and instead talked to the local paper in the hope of stirring outrage in the community. I advised her to call the project The Sicilian Vespas. The paper published an article calling her The Biking Boadicea, with a photo of her looking fierce, her jutting chin in the foreground. The thefts continued.

Soon afterwards we moved to Spitalfields, where you can hang on to your vehicle for a bit longer. Fluffy now became set on buying a motorbike and sidecar. She would ride the bike, she asserted, and I would sit in the sidecar with our cat Maud. She talked of equipping Maud with a small helmet and perhaps a scarf, and, to soften me up, invited me to imagine her (Maud's) whiskers blowing in the breeze, like the moustache of a flying ace in World War I. Waving aside my objection that such vehicles had, for good reason, fallen out of use (in the family album there is a photo, from the 1920s, of my maternal grandfather in the saddle, with my grandmother and infant mother where Maud and I would be), Fluffy phoned a specialist manufacturer to inquire about a bespoke job. When he asked which side she wanted the sidecar, she replied that the right-hand side would be nice – which meant that, in Britain, her overtakings would have swung Maud and me into the path of oncoming traffic that Fluffy couldn't see. The price the man quoted was huge, the secondhand alternatives were decrepit, and so Fluffy moved on to her next fad, which was non-vehicular.

As well as the scooter, she had a pink-and-white Citroën 2CV, which she called Dolly. It may have been the name of the model, but Fluffy had turned it into the name of the particular car. I am irritated by the whimsicality of naming your car, an affectation more common among girls than boys – although my friend Hamish called his The Dominator. My mother's Triumph Mayflower had been christened Buttercup, which created floral confusion. It is said that the 2CV was designed for French farmers, and that you could carry a sheep in one, as Egyptians carry theirs on scooters. A sheep might have found Dolly agreeable, but to me the car was grotty. Rust had eaten through the floor: as you drove along, you could see the tarmac whizzing under you – just as, when you flushed the lavatory in an old railway carriage, you could see the ballast on to which your waste fell with a trickle of water. Fluffy being chaotic, Dolly was strewn with abandoned pizzas, snotty tissues, dirty tights, and surprising items such as a plastic turquoise alarm clock in the form of a mosque. At the set time, it would light up and a scratchily recorded muezzin would call you to prayer. I got a fright the first time it happened.

The heaps of rubbish caused bickering when,

the day after our wedding, we were driving down Shoreditch High Street. Having previously complained that the ring Fluffy had bought for me was too big, I waggled my left hand to show how it rattled on my finger, but instead it flew off. As we sifted the heaps in search of it, I improvised variations on 'Yuck' and 'Euuuugh', while she told me to shut up and reminded me that, had I not been so childish as to wave my hand around, I would not be getting it sticky now. The sifting having produced only acrimony, we concluded that the ring had fallen through a rust hole in the floor, and so we walked slowly back along the street, peering at the gutter, with no greater success. Months later, Fluffy found the ring under what remained of the carpet. It had been held there by a piece of chewed gum.

Dolly was a pain to drive. One problem was that she refused unleaded petrol. Fluffy sometimes had ready a vial of special stuff – lead, I suppose – which she would pour into the tank after buying petrol; but that was a palaver, and anyway the vial was usually empty. In that case we would drive in a forlorn quest for a lead-petrol vendor, while the fuel gauge pressed further into the red. Then there was the heterodox order of the gears, reverse being where fourth should be. If you selected reverse by mistake, the car didn't fly backwards, but there would be a ghastly grinding. When I caused this to happen, Fluffy would accuse me of maliciously wrecking the gearbox. Once you were in fourth, you only tootled along, for Dolly was not a performance car, unless 'performance' includes 'poor performance'. She was less a *deux chevaux* than a *demi-mulet*. The engine sounded like, and may have been, a lawn mower's.

The panels, which dented if you leant against them, may have been of cardboard or papier mâché. Dolly was so flimsy that you would have thought twice about committing your sheep to her. I feared having my legs crushed when Fluffy was at the wheel, for, the car being narrow, my wife enjoyed squeezing into spaces between buses and lorries, as she did on the scooter. She is a skilful motorist, but her skill is of the sort you find at Brands Hatch or in Naples:[1] she drives aggressively, swerving between lanes, cutting in front of other drivers – whom she then insultingly thanks with two flashes of the lights – and, when there is a jam ahead, zooming back down the street in reverse. Fluffy is oblivious of traffic lights and one-way signs, but her oblivion is studied – unlike that of my self-important friend the Hon Felicity Greaves, who, when a taxi driver called her a dozy cow for absentmindedly driving me and some others the wrong way down Pall Mall, clearly hoped that none of us had heard. '*Not* a dozy cow,' Felicity mooed to herself.

If other road users show Fluffy the contempt she shows them, she is enraged, but she is usually the cause of road rage in someone else. The situation is made worse by her responding in double measure, and so the thing escalates, as journalists say of political conflicts. There is shouting, fist-shaking,

---

[1] When I was in a Neapolitan taxi, the driver took a short cut along a railway line, the car juddering over the sleepers, *à la* Keystone Cops.

the calling of terrible names, and the threat of violence. Even the mildest protest sets her off. 'Get off the road, you wanker!' she bawled at a young cyclist who had frowned at her. 'You should be ashamed of using such language at your age,' he replied. My mother, when much older, had called someone a wanker, but she was excused, having picked the word up from me, by not knowing what it meant. On another occasion Fluffy got into some argy with a father who was driving his two little girls to school in a Range Rover. The girls were sitting side by side in the back, wearing blazers and boaters. When the man drove off, angrily swinging his car in front of ours, the girls lost balance, their boaters rocking in unison.

Such incidents leave me shaky when I am in the car, for, although there has never been actual violence, we have come close to it, and I, as the male, am the likely whipping boy. The closest we came was when Fluffy was parking Dolly outside a church, where we were to attend a memorial service. Hamish was in the back of the car, where the sheep would go. Unseen by any of us, a white van had been making for the same space. Its driver, a large skinhead with tattoos, swaggered up to Fluffy's window and shouted 'That's my space, you cow. Get out before I put my fist through your roof!' Hamish and I murmured to Fluffy that, even though her mistake had been innocent, it might be best to yield; but she sprang from the car and launched a Philippic at the skinhead, jabbing his chest, which was level with her head. I slid down in my seat.

Hamish, a powerful but pacific man, put his head in his hands. After half a minute of this, the skinhead returned to his van, fulminating but beaten. As he receded, Fluffy shouted 'Cunt!' after him, which was pushing her luck. We were in the wrong mood for the memorial service.

That evening, as we drove home from the supper given by the bereaved, Fluffy got into an argument with the owner of a Porsche, at whom she had flicked a V sign. He looked familiar, and I thought that he might be a legal colleague or a client. The row developed into a dodgem ride, each trying to force the other off the road. Given the cars involved, it is, in a way, to Fluffy's credit that, with a sudden swing into the path of the Porsche, she made it scrape its front wheel against the kerb. As it then gave chase, she drove to the nearest police station. When we stopped there, her opponent peeled off, but by now I was so disgusted that I took a taxi the rest of the way home. I threatened then, as I often have, never to let Fluffy drive me again, but she knows the threat to be empty, the convenience of a private chauffeur outweighing the risk of being intentionally thumped or accidentally mangled.

Had the incident occurred a few months later, I would have been swapping one taxi for another. When Dolly's floor became so crumbly with rust that we had to hold our feet in the air (good for the thighs), Fluffy conceded that it was time for the car to be replaced. An old taxi was the thing, she announced, having cherished the one she had bought, years before, to ferry her stroke-stricken father and his wheelchair. She enjoyed parking in the Disabled spaces outside Tesco and, when her father died, was tempted to continue using them, feigning a funny walk to avert rebukes. We both recognise that this would be shameful, but are happy to go to the checkout with the wide aisle for wheelchair users. 'I hope you're disabled!' shouted a woman from the longer queue at the neighbouring aisle. 'It's not *only* for disabled people,' I replied. 'You're *mentally* disabled,' she called back. There was some sniggering among the queuers. It blossomed into guffaws when I contemptuously leant against my trolley, which slid away, causing me to fall over and prove the woman's point.

The taxi to buy, according to Fluffy, was a Fairway. There was a wide choice on eBay. She was attracted by a yellow one in Nottingham, but I didn't fancy the trip there to collect it, and, as I knew from several visits, Nottingham taxis have a sign inside saying 'Penalty for soiling: fifty pounds'. The odd fare might have a dog who is caught short, but the warning is presumably directed at binge-drinking pukers. You could remove the sign, of course, but the memory would remain, and in any event a black cab was more stylish and discreet. Restricting our search to black Fairways in Greater London, we bought one in Romford – Greater London at a stretch – for £2,000. Since a new taxi costs tens of thousands, it was a bargain, although I pointed out to Fluffy that ours was eight years old and had 160,000 miles on the clock. That was nothing, she assured me: taxis went to the moon and back before they conked out. I imagined a rank on the moon, with one of those green wooden huts into which the drivers like to squash to drink Camp Coffee and Bovril.

We missed the sights of Romford, for the seller – a cabby who was retiring to Spain – offered to drive the taxi to our house and show us the works. When he drew up, his wife was in the back. Fat, pink and dreamy, she reminded me of a comical inflatable lady that my father had once bought.[2] The cabby had not mentioned that he was taking his wife to Spain, so I asked whether she was included in the sale. 'Don't tempt me,' he replied, while she continued to smile gormlessly. She seemed not to be all there.

Fluffy and I each had a go, with the cabby supervising from one of the folding seats behind. The driving seat was high, enabling one to gaze contumeliously down on car drivers, as cabbies do, but the controls were primitive, and the gears as odd as Dolly's: the transmission was mainly automatic, but to get into top gear you had to reach down and press a button which extinguished a small green light. As Fairways do not have a front passenger seat, Fluffy talked of installing one, but I was against the idea: if as usual she was driving, I could stretch out in the back, shut the connecting window, to exclude her

---

[2] Fluffy gave me a pair of inflatable antlers, which I hung on my office wall; they leaked and went flaccid after a few days, prompting ribald comments from colleagues. The only other ornament in my office was an open-heart mouse pad, which I had bought at the Body Worlds exhibition. There was mock blood inside, which you could squish around, but eventually the covering plastic perished and the blood leaked out, clogging the wheel of the mouse.

artless prattle and her yells at other motorists, and read in peace. It would be better than a public taxi, for most of these, unlike our cab, have intercoms enabling the driver to natter to the passenger. I always switch the intercom off, but, if the cabby is a resolute natterer, he can switch it on again, in which case you have to hide behind your paper or fiddle with your phone. Even that will not deter the hardest nuts. Fearing that Fluffy might be offended by my preference, I expressed it in terms of preserving the integrity of the design, and she affected to believe me. She asserted that the taxi was to be called Maxi, and that this was a female name. Are the names of cars, like those of ships, usually female? Why? Was 'The Dominator' a female name?

The advantages of owning a taxi are many. There is the famous turning-circle, which I came to take for granted, so that when driving other vehicles I had some nasty scrapes, literally. You also join the select band who use taxis as private cars – Prince Philip, Stephen Fry and other national treasures. Then there is the uncanny courtesy of real taxi drivers: scornful of ordinary motorists, they preserve honour with each other and, if they think you are one of the family, will smilingly wave you on – kicking themselves only when they see that your cab lacks a licence plate on the back. Private users are forbidden to keep the plate – the same applies to the 'For Hire' light – and Fluffy unscrewed ours in a moment of conformism. They are also, of course, forbidden to drive in the lanes reserved for taxis and buses, but it is a risk worth taking, so great is the saving of time and stress, and so small the danger of being caught. Only the absence of the licence plate betrays you, and only the most alert observer notices that it is missing. We were caught once, when stuck in front of a bus, the driver of which took a photo, but we laughed off the fine as a fair tax.

Maxi was useful to me at work, Fluffy giving me a lift to or from the office when I had bulky documents to carry. She could have done so in almost any vehicle, but the cab created a businesslike impression. I had boasted about it to my boss, who was hurrying out of the building just as we drew up. 'That's my cab,' I said to him as we passed on the pavement. 'Ah, great,' he replied in a fluster, leapt in and instructed Fluffy to take him to King's Cross. His smile was pinched when she booted him out. She collected me one evening after a visit to Spitalfields market, where she had bought a ventriloquist's dummy whom she summarily christened Colin. Nattily dressed in a tweed jacket with plus-twos and brogue shoes, and jauntily holding a wooden cigarette between two fingers, Colin was let down only by his nylon wig, which looked like a Beatles mop. He had been going cheap because his mouth no longer moved – he should have been the ventriloquist – but you could get his eyes to swivel. I didn't notice him as I got into the cab, and it was only once I had sat down that I found him next to me, snugly seatbelted. It was too shocking to be funny.

Fluffy and Maxi served me well on the day the police shot that Brazilian at Stockwell station, causing the Tube to shut down and all the real taxis to be snapped up. Stranded with clients at Elephant and Castle, I told them I would ring for my private one, and they were impressed when Fluffy rolled up in Maxi twenty minutes later. Their admiration dwindled on closer inspection of the cab, which was so filthy that local youths had written 'Clean Me' and 'Fuck' in the dust. A hub cap was missing, and inside the passenger compartment there was a pile of old bricks – something to do with Fluffy's interior-design business. Having dropped us back in the City, Fluffy drove around offering lifts to other stranded travellers, who desperately hailed her. She did so out of kindness, explaining that Maxi was a private car and declining payment. That seemed to me over-scrupulous, and I was pleased that she made an exception for a bunch of Goldman Sachs men, whom she charged 200 pounds to drive to City airport. She told me that she met some interesting types among her passengers, but that she was startled by the high-handedness of some, who had quickly forgotten that she was a hostess and not a cabby. It put her off doing The Knowledge, a project with which she had toyed (along with joining the Foreign Legion, opening a brothel, and breeding hedgehogs as pets).

That folk often think you are a proper taxi driver is one of the disadvantages. I would not be ashamed to earn my living that way, but I didn't want to be tainted with the reputation of cabbies for garrulous bigotry. There is some truth in it. One of them, who, having overridden my silencing of the intercom, was drivelling on about the police, said 'Of course, the British police are the best in the world.' I asked him why he thought so. He paused, eyed me narrowly in the mirror, decided to ignore my question, and continued ranting. Cabbies also have a reputation, less justified, for surliness: it is perhaps a hangover from the days of the horse-drawn cab, when they had to sit out on the box in the rain – enough to make anyone surly. I likewise made allowances for the stone-deaf driver who made me write down my destination; I scribbled 'Percy Street W1', he took me to Parfrey Street W6, and, when I protested in improvised sign language, he told me that my writing would shame a GP. I chose to smile, for Dr Johnson was right that deafness is one of the most desperate of human calamities, and our journey to the wrong street had been refreshingly chat-free.

I have been sterner in other cases, as with the buffoon who drove his taxi over a nail-ridden plank. This having buggered the front wheels, he told me to get out and demanded the fare to that point. In the face of this rudeness, and bearing in mind that it was raining and after midnight, I replied that he had contracted to take me home, and that, since he had not done so, I would pay him nothing. The cabby replied that I was a thieving gurrier. Instead of asking what a gurrier was, I countered that I was a solicitor and knew what was what. Although I was, I didn't: at law school we had been given a lecture on quantum meruit, but I could not now remember the doctrine. As I strutted off into the gloom, expecting to be rugby-tackled, or to be hit on the back of the head by a missile, I realised that he had dropped me two minutes' walk from my flat.

Fluffy and I were often asked whether it was a bore being hailed, but that was not much of a problem – first because, there being no 'For Hire' light, hailings were rare, and secondly because you could always ignore the hailer. If he or she was a deserving case, such as the orthopaedically shod old lady I passed in (oddly) a hail storm, I would smile apologetically. A more frequent embarrassment was to be asked for directions. It usually happened when you were waiting at traffic lights. Just as they were turning green, the man in the car next to you would slowly wind down his window, say 'Excuse me, mate,' and ask the way to Catford. Fluffy's stock reply, as the cars behind started to hoot, was that she was not a taxi driver and didn't know. If the man took in only the bit about not knowing, he would tell her that she called herself a cabby; if he noticed the 'I'm not a taxi driver', he would ask her what she called the thing she was driving. At that point Fluffy would have one of her turns. To avoid such expense of spirit, I, if at the wheel, would make up some directions; but, if they were too wide of the mark, the questioner would catch me out, and the dialectic would run along similar lines. There were other misunderstandings. When Fluffy, who was driving me somewhere, was talking rubbish while we waited at the lights, I leant forward and playfully throttled her through the connecting window. There were astonished looks from the driver and the passenger in the taxi beside us. Perhaps the latter longed for the nerve to do the same to the former, who had also been blathering away.

Fairways are crude vehicles, with few comforts and no suspension. They are fitted with heaters, but ours, although fierce in the driver's compartment, merely whirred loudly in the passenger's. Opening the connecting window to equalise the temperature was no good, for the driver roasted before the passenger thawed. I was annoyed that the radio too was on the blink, often though I had wished for that in hired cabs, where a phone-in about football is usually the main alternative to the driver's idle talk. Once I was startled to recognise on the radio the voice of my high-minded friend Brian: the phone-in turned out to be on philosophy, and he was fielding the questions, under the tutelage of a DJ who was determined to make a joke of it all. The callers were especially keen on the wisdom of the East, about which Brian, an analytic philosopher of logic, knew no more than they. My cabby got bored with it and switched to Capital Gold. Perhaps he had once had that Bertrand Russell in the back.

Fairways are also heavy, and so they gulp fuel – a problem aggravated, in our case, by Fluffy's neglect of the gauge. When she got round to casting a glance at it, or I paternalistically stretched forward from the back to check it myself, the needle was often beyond the red bit and pressed against E, whereupon there would be panic and harsh words. When we ran dry in a street used by buses for parking, Fluffy ordered me to stay in Maxi while she went in search of diesel. The cab, too heavy for us to push to the kerb, was stuck in the middle of the road, and the buses had to squeeze round it. That was beyond the skill of one driver, a combustible West Indian, who banged on my window and repeatedly shouted 'Where de cabby!' I pulled the window down and, with chilly courtesy masking my fear, told him the situation, explaining that this was a private car. Equally unskilled at processing information, or perhaps just unwilling to do so, he resumed his tirade, and so I slammed the window up again, locked it, and pretended to read the paper, while he continued to shout and gesticulate. When my wife returned with a can, he rounded on her, provoking a vintage Fluffy response. At the climax, the man was bellowing that we were white trash. Fluffy flagged down a police car and demanded that he be arrested for racial abuse. The policemen drove off, shaking their heads sadly.

In central London, Maxi's virtues outshone her vices; on long trips out of town it was the other way round, as we discovered when we bought a cottage in West Dorset.[3] In a normal car the journey takes three-and-a-half hours, but with Maxi you needed to add an hour – and to make sure that you had enough in your current account to pay for the filling of her tank. We had the customary panic with the fuel gauge late one night on Salisbury Plain, soon after

---

[3] Our friend Ruth sent an email to her friend Jeremy in a village near ours: 'You must meet the lovely Blacks, I'm sure you'll get on.' Jeremy replied 'Let's hope they're not like all the other bloody boring lawyers who buy second homes in West Dorset, pushing up the prices and driving out the locals.' Ruth, who likes to stir, forwarded the reply to me, and I thought of writing to this Jeremy that I was an Identikit replica of the lawyers in question. When Fluffy and I met him and his wife for drinks at Ruth's, we all gushed.

Maud had been sick in her basket beside me. I pictured her, Fluffy and me kipping under the stones of the Henge and then being rescued by an armoured car on its way back from nocturnal manoeuvres to one of the bases nearby.

Maxi excited comment in our village, the tenor being one of condescending amusement. I found our neighbour, a retired surveyor, smiling wryly at the cab. 'Are your tyres cross-ply or radial?' he asked, his eyebrows raised. I beamed and shrugged. He squatted down by the front wheel. 'Cross-ply,' he sighed gleefully. 'You'll never get here in the winter on those: you won't make it up the hill.' This exchange took place in January. I decided to let him work it out for himself.

You could get Maxi up to eighty on the open road, but it took several minutes to do so. Acceleration was so leisurely that if you pulled out to overtake, and the road then started to climb a gentle hill, the slowcoach you were trying to pass would gain on you, and you would be trapped in the middle of the road, facing oncoming lorries. Navigation was also hard. The absence of an intercom, normally a blessing, made it hard for Fluffy to hear me when I shouted directions from the back, so she would urge me to perch behind her on one of the folding seats. This I resisted because, in the first place, it made me feel sick to face backwards; in the second, the folding seats lacked belts – a concern, given Fluffy's driving style; and, in the third, they were uncomfortable. (It was a cruel prank, played on Japanese tourists some years ago, to tell them that in a hired taxi they had to sit on the folding seats unless they paid extra.) The result was that mis-hearings abounded, tempers frayed and, until we had mastered the route to our new house, the journey took even longer. We left one roundabout by the road from which we had entered it, not discovering the mistake until, twenty miles back, things started looking familiar. There is a rebuttable presumption, when you get lost, that it's the fault of the navigator; I would try to rebut it by shouting 'I told you to go LEFT!' and reminding Fluffy that, even when staring at her hands, she has trouble distinguishing left from right. She was deaf to my arguments, as she was to my directions.

In a way I admire my friend Dan, who, when fed up with navigating, simply shuts the atlas and either lights a fag or nods off, unmoved by remonstrations from the driver. It's an instance of his general languor as a passenger. When, at a difficult T-junction, his wife Amelia, who was driving us, asked Dan to look to the left while she looked to the right, he said 'OK, clear now,' as a lorry bore down on us. I screamed as Amelia started to pull into its path, and she jerked to a halt. 'I meant OK after this lorry,' Dan added, unruffled.

Some problems have been eased by the satnav, but I dislike the device because, unlike an old-fashioned map, it obscures the big picture of the route. It can also play up. When Mike, another friend, was driving me back from Wales, we stopped for a pee at a motorway service station; as we stood in a row of men at the urinal, the satnav, which Mike had put in his back pocket, suddenly said 'Turn round as soon as possible.'[4] It is, however, a boon if you have weak eyes. I have been short-sighted since childhood, and since my forties I have been long-sighted; it was a blow to discover that the conditions are not mutually exclusive. I therefore need different spectacles for seeing road signs and for reading maps, and I can never change them quickly enough – the attempt petering out into peevish fumbling. Varifocals would solve the problem, but they are a marker of senility: if you wear them, you probably wear a hearing aid. My solution, which reduces to one the number of pairs of glasses in play, is to read the map with my bare eyes, holding it two inches from my nose. Fluffy ridicules me, but she, being only long-sighted, can make out nothing at close range. Maud is the same.

My eyesight is especially bad at night. Once it gets dusk, I can see the road ahead only if there are

[4] Less entertaining was the tour of north-east London on which Fluffy's device took us when we were driving what should have been half a mile from a cinema to a new Turkish restaurant on the Kingsland Road. We were testy when we arrived, for we had wanted only a quick kebab before bed, and our temper didn't improve when we realised that we faced a choice between sitting at the back, which smelt of Dettol, or at the front, by the charcoal grill – atmospheric, you might think, for you could watch the chef ply the kebabs like a virtuoso xylophonist; but over the grill was an extractor fan, the roar of which, like that of a jumbo taking off, precluded conversation. Long married by then, we settled for a no-talking supper. The next time we went Turkish on the Kingsland Road, we lit on the haunt of Gilbert and George. There they were in their matching suits. Fluffy and I talked of adopting matching gear in a different style and of making a point of sitting across the aisle from G and G at every meal. Would it faze them? Might we too become celebrities? I can't draw a convincing picture of an ejaculating knob, but Fluffy is artistic.

street lights or the headlights are on full beam. The latter provokes retaliatory flashes from oncoming vehicles, which make me blinder still. If I am driving in the country at night, I crawl along till a car overtakes me, and then I follow its tail lights, like a partially-sighted Paralympic skiier. The result is that I am usually going more quickly or more slowly than I want to. The method presupposes that the man in front can see more than I; if not, his overtaking was a wild gamble. Sometimes, my mind on other things, I will follow him when he turns off my route, and I end up in the sticks, unable to see my way back.

On your driving test you have to read a registration plate at twenty metres, but the requirement is poorly enforced: when I took my test, I needed new glasses, and I got through only because the examiner had an absurdly modest idea of twenty metres. In any case, your eyesight can deteriorate later. Harriet, an elderly friend who often muddles her spectacles, was driving me and her husband Ernest at high speed along a busy road when she breezily said 'I can't think what I've done with my other glasses – I can't see a thing through these.' Ernest exploded; a bishop, he strains to avoid illegality or even impropriety, a fact that may explain why, when we walked past a sex shop in a Norfolk village, he pretended not to have noticed it, and strode on while I peered through the window. The establishment was deserted. A local told me that it had always been busy when it had been a tea shop.

When Ernest and Harriet came to dinner, I offered them a parking space in the yard behind our house. The yard is entered through a narrow arch, their car was wide, and Harriet, who as usual was driving, was worried about scratches; so I stood at the front, waving a bit to the left, a bit to the right, and so on. Perhaps because she had the wrong glasses on, she failed to follow my simple instructions, and scraped a two-foot strip of paint off the passenger door. A proud woman, she blamed me, and there was an atmosphere over dinner. The next time they visited, I left them to find a space for themselves in the street. For no good reason, they parked in a Disabled bay; while they were eating in our house, the bay's rightful user emptied two tins of minestrone over the car. The evening ended with buckets, sponges, Fairy Liquid and brittle laughter. Ernest and Harriet have not visited us since.

The minestrone-emptier has a large Mercedes, adapted for hands-only driving. It's a far cry from the stigmatising pale-blue tricycles – called Invacars, to rub it in – to which disabled drivers were condemned when I was a boy. Inside there was room for only one person and a wheelchair, the assumption presumably being that a cripple has no friends. One of these vehicles had signs on the front and the back saying 'CAUTION: NO HAND SIGNALS. VEHICLE DRIVEN WITH FEET.' I was too frightened to look inside. In our more accommodating age, even severely disabled people can drive. A young man at my office, barely able to move, would be lowered at COB, by his carer, from an electric wheelchair into the driving seat of a Lotus, and off they would roar.

Well before completing her return journey from the moon, Maxi began to emit a grinding noise and a burning smell, so I drove her to a garage specialising in taxis. On the way, the exhaust pipe started to belch smoke so dense that other drivers hooted and pedestrians pointed, waved and laughed. When I got there, I could not stop the motor, which was now revving madly. Jeff, the garagiste, who would normally soothe you with his catchphrase 'Don't panic, mechanic,' sucked his teeth, said he had never seen anything like it, and told me to wait in his office – a windowless cave under a railway arch – while he tried to cut off the fuel supply. To keep Maxi's smoke out, I shut the office door behind me and settled down behind Jeff's desk to leaf through his *Men Only*. Hardly had my loins stirred when I noticed that smoke was welling up from under the door, so I decided to go back into the yard. The door would not open. As the fumes thickened, I hammered and yelled, but Maxi's shriek, which was rising in volume and pitch, and was now overlaid with the sound of approaching sirens, drowned my cries. I was resigning myself to brain-damage or death when the motor stopped and Jeff's lad rescued me. As I reeled gasping into the yard, three fire engines, summoned by an officious bystander, pulled up and twelve firemen, in fetching yellow trousers, sprang out and started running around. They were confused and irked by the lack of a fire, and I thought that, like Matilda's aunt, I would have to pay to get the men to go away.

I left Maxi's remains with Jeff, who gave me

twenty pounds for scrap. That evening Fluffy and I considered our next vehicle. Her suggestions included a double-decker bus, a milk float, and one of those three-wheelers that say 'Mr Coffee, He's So Frothy'. Reminding her that we now shuttled up and down the A303, I insisted on something sensible. She told me I meant 'boring'. There followed an exchange of rhetoric, at the end of which Fluffy, conceding the point of substance, asserted that, if I was determined to be an old fart, we were to have a Honda Jazz. An online search for used ones revealed that the further from London they were, the cheaper they got, the best trade-off between price and distance being in Wigan. We found Wigan on the map and, noticing that it was not by the sea, decided that Orwell had been an idiot for thinking that it had a pier. The car in question, the advertisement told us, had had only one careful owner. Fluffy, dismissing my observation that 'only one careful owner' was consistent with 'many careless owners', marched off to catch a train to Wigan, and returned that evening with the Jazz. She has since admitted that, after Maxi, it is the acme of luxury. (Her word was 'acne', but the meaning was clear.) There is suspension, the heater and the radio work, you can climb hills, the fuel gauge stays on F for hours, and passenger and driver can sit side by side, conversing freely. If you buy anything fancier, you're a patsy.

Pets to Avoid

Before we got our cat, Fluffy and I considered other kinds of pet (or 'non-human animal companion', if you are concerned not to offend). Ideas ranged from the unwise to the dotty. At the latter end of the spectrum was Fluffy's suggestion that we adopt a saltwater crocodile, which she said would be called Nipper. Perhaps she hoped to bounce me into getting an animal I knew little about, but I had encountered crocs – possibly not the saltwater variety, but it made no odds – at the zoo. One I tried, and failed, to beat in a who-blinks-first competition; I don't know whether they have eyelids. In any case, information was readily available from Wikipedia, which said that the saltwater crocodile could grow to 5.2 metres and 1,000 kilograms, that it was capable of taking on any animal in its territory, and that it was the most dangerous crocodilian to humans. That seemed to settle the matter, but Fluffy was persistent. The conversation ran as follows. F: 'He can live in the bath.' O: 'He will be too big for the bath.' F: 'He can curl up, or hang over the edge.' O: 'The taps don't run with salt water.' F: 'We can add bath salts.' O: 'That's the wrong kind of salt.' F: 'We've got Saxa in the kitchen.' O: 'What happens when I want a bath?' F: 'Nipper can wait in the shower.' O: 'He will eat us alive.' F: 'We can file his teeth down.' This last suggestion was as fanciful as the advice issued by the Burmese authorities when floods enabled crocodiles to escape from Rangoon zoo: if you are confronted with one, slide a sack over its head.

Reading our conversation out of context, you might think that Fluffy was a small child rather than a matron in her forties, and that it would have been more dignified of me not to stoop to discussion; but the only way to dislodge her whims is, as business people say, to 'push back'. At first she defends the whim ferociously, taking the line that anyone who disagrees is a halfwit, but then it suddenly evaporates, and she is on to the next one. So it was with Nipper. Fluffy settled for a small stuffed alligator, which she found in the Spitalfields bric-à-brac market. She is on good terms with the taxidermy man there, who phones her in advance when he has something special; last week it was a polar bear, which I vetoed. The head and front legs of the alligator peep out from under our sofa, startling our more nervous guests.

We ruled out other aquatic creatures. My late friend Milo (Olim Milo) had the devil of a time installing warty newts (*Triturus Cristatus*) in his pond: the problem was not the newts but their breeder, a

Barbara Woodhouse of the amphibian world, who would not release them without visiting the pond and interrogating Milo on their future welfare. She also made heavy weather of the useless fact that 'a newt' derives from 'an ewt' – like 'an orange' from 'a norange', but with the 'n' moving in the other direction. Obviously such a person would not allow her newts or ewts to be kept in the bath, like poor Nipper, and Fluffy and I do not have a pond.

I floated a goldfish (so to speak), having happy memories of one called Funny, whom I won at a fair when I was five. He thrived until we bought him a smart but sickly bowl-mate, called Finny, from Harrods. In the hope of pepping Finny up, my father put a teaspoonful of brandy in the water – the idea of our doctor, who was visiting for another reason. The following morning we found Funny gazing up at Finny's corpse, which was drifting on the surface. Grief, infection or alcohol-poisoning did for Funny too, and we buried both of them in the window box.

Fluffy said that goldfish were boring and gave her the creeps. She was still hankering after a reptile, so I proposed a tortoise – more controllable than a crocodile. Older readers may remember Fred, the tortoise on *Blue Peter.* John Noakes painted the name on the shell, and had to squash an A on the end when the animal was found to be female.[1] At my nursery school there was a tortoise called Winston who was attached to a fence by a piece of string; one day, when

---

[1] They got into worse trouble with the 'Paint Your Dog' competition, some young viewers applying Dulux to their dogs.

he was tied to a different post, my friends and I dropped stones on his usual site, causing our teacher to rush out in alarm. We thought it hilarious. A little girl at the school had a tortoise of her own, which she used to dress up in doll's clothes and wheel around in a miniature perambulator; the old face peering out of a frilly collar made her laugh and frightened her playmates who looked into the pram. Years later I knew a tortoise called Nonsense, who, mistaking my brown brogue shoe for a female of his species, clambered on and gave it a good going over. It was on my foot at the time. I was touched but not aroused. Perhaps girl tortoises feel rather more.

Fluffy gave thought to this proposal. We had once stayed at a hotel in Fez, and she had liked the tortoises that mooched around the courtyard there. They were easy to miss: one I unwittingly kicked across the yard, and there must have been a crushing or two every season. Perhaps they were turned into soup when that happened. Fluffy borrowed one to put in our bed, but it seemed anxious there. Research revealed two obstacles to our having a tortoise as a pet. One was that in summer the animals needed more sunlight than reached the terrace of our London house. The garden of our country cottage was bright enough, but who would look after the tortoise when we were not there? It could not be asked to travel back and forth, like a cat in a basket, and it would become torpid during its stays in London. The other obstacle was that tortoises were no longer readily available for sale, and we knew no one with a hand-me-down or a clutch of eggs.

This obstacle was pooh-poohed by my cousin Miriam, who had smuggled her own tortoise, Euclid, from Greece in her suitcase. Beryl, Miriam's cat, did not know what to make of Euclid, and tapped him warily with her paw, whereupon he retreated into his yellow shell and waited for her to go away. Euclid was small and lively and, contrary to the saying that tortoises move slowly, would canter about the garden, in search of escape routes. Miriam built an enclosure for him, but one night he worked his way under the chicken wire. She never saw him again.

Before Beryl and Euclid, Miriam had an owl, whom she called Solon, because owls are said to be wise. An ornithologist tells me that this saying too is false. Owls, he asserts, are among the stupidest birds: they look as if they have big heads, with brains to match, but most of the head is feathers, and if you plucked it you would find a stick underneath. Perhaps, but it strikes me as clever, even if not wise, to catch a mouse by plunging on it in the dark from several hundred feet. I'd like to see the ornithologist try it. Whether or not owls are wise, Miriam is an idiot. Her idea was that Solon would sleep in her flat during the day and fly out to hunt at night. That, of course, required her to keep the window open, but one chilly night she shut it and Solon flew into the glass, breaking his neck. She buried him under a tree in Regent's Park.

Such an arrangement can work if you are responsible and attentive. At age sixteen, Bill Dagg, a boy at my boarding school, was the world expert on a rare species of bat that lived in some outbuildings in the school grounds. One of the bats he tamed: by night it would hang out with its friends, and by day it would hang upside down on a rug attached to the wall of Bill's study. Bill had few human visitors, for there were droppings on the seat under the rug, the study was freezing in winter, and a bat is a sinister creature.

Untainted by Miriam's incompetence, Fluffy and I talked of getting a bird. I fancied a crow. Barnaby Rudge had a raven, and a neighbour's daughter has a tame carrion crow which she nursed from its infancy. When the girl is at school, the crow flies there at break time, circles over the playground and, on spotting its mistress, lands on her head. That strikes me as affectionate and intelligent, although my ornithologist might pour cold water on the thought. I am on nodding terms with a carrion crow that walks up and down the parapet outside the window of my study. When it first noticed me, it gave me a beady look as it passed, and, just as it was moving out of my line of vision, it stopped and stared at me again, over its shoulder. 'Never make eye contact with a bird,' a friend told me who, having done so with a thrush, was attacked by it; but the crow and I rub along well.

I suggested to Fluffy that we try to tame it, but she, like Edgar Allan Poe, sees a crow as a thing of evil, and said that, if we were to have a bird, we would do better to think of a budgerigar – a nice blue one. If we were to have a budgie, I retorted, it would have to be green; but I did not fancy one of either colour. My aunt's budgie, Pepin, was noisy and highly strung.

His cage was on top of the fridge, which hummed, as fridges do. One day there was a power cut, the humming stopped, and Pepin died. It made me wonder whether there is some background sound or vibration which I don't notice but on which I similarly depend. Then there is the fire risk: it may be an urban myth, but I am inclined to believe the story about the budgie that broke its leg, had a match as a splint, and combusted after hopping on to the sandpaper at the bottom of its cage. If that had happened to Pepin, I could have made the joke about the Serious Burns Unit, for he liked to say 'Wee, sleekit, cow'rin, tim'rous beastie'. I don't know why my aunt taught him that line.

The talking was part of a budgerigar's attraction for Fluffy, and for the same reason she looked favourably on parrots. I pointed out that it was amusing at first but got you down after a while, and that a parrot might pick up various sounds that you did not want repeated. My friend Hamish lived in a flat above a parrot that imitated a phone conversation: it would ring a few times, then say 'Hallo' in the voice of its mistress, then carry on some nonsensical chat, then say 'Well, goodbye' in the same voice, and make the noise of a receiver being hung up. If in the mood, it would repeat this sequence many times, with only half a minute's interval between. When it got bored, it would emit random rings, and then subside into tuneless whistling. I don't know how Hamish put up with it.

Or take the house down the road from us in the country, in which live a parrot and a big dog. The former occupies a cage by the front window and, when you walk past, the latter barks through the window, standing with its front legs sprawled over the top of the cage. The parrot takes this in its stride, and has recently started to bark too, with a tinnier timbre. Nay, more: I once worked as a temp typist in an office with a heavy smoker and his parrot. The bird imitated not only its master's phlegmy cough, but also the sound of footsteps approaching along the corridor, a knock on the door, and the master saying 'Come in.' I didn't know whether I was coming or going.

The champion imitators are mynas, one of which I encountered in a bird sanctuary. Having received many visitors, it had picked up various accents. 'Hellay, hi ye?' (hallo, how are you) it greeted me in the voice of a Hooray Henry. This distortion of vowels – presumably meant, by humans, to signify a smiling mouth – is trickling down the middle class, more and more of whom are unsmilingly saying 'phane' for 'phone', 'feed' for 'food', and 'gid' for 'good'. The myna then swung into Cockney: 'Y'or'roigh?' (you all right), it asked. Unable to keep up with this, I tried teaching it to say 'Oliver'. After a few minutes it was getting close, and talking like me.

Mynas are a kind of starling, and the garden-variety starling too is a promiscuous imitator. Taking a stroll in Kensington Gardens to compose myself before the first exam of my Law Society Finals, I heard one quacking in the tree above me. Not realising that starlings could imitate ducks, I feared that the strain of revision was causing a hallucination, and so the walk failed to have the intended effect. The quacking was a bit tinny, like the barking of my neighbour's parrot.

Very well, said Fluffy: if we couldn't have a talking bird, what about a useful one? She suggested a turkey. I rejected this, first, because I find turkey meat boring and, second, because live turkeys are hideous and alien. I have a PTSD-type memory of visiting a turkey shed when a child: the floor was a heaving grey sea of birds, one of which, mad with claustrophobia, was running in a tight circle and screaming. The memory resurfaced when Fluffy and I visited a rare-breeds farm, where there was a long row of pens, each containing a turkey of a different kind. When we approached, the one in the nearest pen started gobbling, which set off the next one, and so on in domino fashion, till they all gobbled in chorus.

I felt more warmly towards the farm's exotic chickens, which had such exuberant ruffs of feathers at the top of their necks that they seemed to be the headless ones of the cliché. How about some of those, I said to Fluffy. If we had hens, she replied, we would need a cock to go with them. In that case, I said, hens were out, for I also had a bad memory of a cock. A girlfriend had taken me to stay with a gay couple who had bought an old farmhouse near Bologna. They kept hens – more for fun than for eggs, as these could never be found in the overgrown garden – and a strutting, polychromatic cock. I was puzzling this bird, by making broody clucking noises at it, when one of our hosts walked up in a pair of tight white jeans. 'I'm admiring your cock,' I heard myself say, and he gave me a sly smile. You can understand why Americans prefer to say 'rooster'. That night I found the cock less admirable. Contrary to popular belief, cocks start to crow not at dawn but in the pitch-dark middle of the night. This one got going, just outside our window, at three-thirty a.m., perhaps to pay me back for pretending to be a hen. Each time I began to nod off again, it would give another fanfare. My girlfriend made things worse by snoring through the lot. 'You look grey, sweetie,' our host with the sly smile said to me over breakfast; 'didn't you sleep well?' I made some tactful comments about the cock. 'Don't worry,' he replied, 'you'll be fine tonight. One quickly becomes cock-deaf.' It was half-true: I slept through the following night, but had dreams about people with raucous voices.

The discussion of poultry led Fluffy and me to ponder other farm animals. The rare-breeds place had a splendid hairy sow, but she would have fallen through our floor, so we turned our minds to miniature varieties. Fluffy found on YouTube a piglet the size of a teacup, but further inquiry revealed that it could grow to a weight of 150 kilos. The RSPCA leaflet *Pigs as Pets*, which opened with the words 'We strongly advise people not to try to keep pigs', taught us a number of disheartening facts, including: (1) pigs suffer from scaly skin, which should be treated with baby oil; (2) if you want to take your pig for a walk, you must keep it on a lead, and you have to stick to a route agreed with the local

Animal Health Office. We doubted that such an office existed in Spitalfields; if not, did that mean that you could walk your pig *ad libitum*, or that you could not walk it at all? If we did need to fix a route, where would the pig like to go? Brick Lane, perhaps, or the Hawksmoor church? It was all too complicated.

In the 1960s there was a craze for mini donkeys, which seemed to be allowed to walk wherever the owners fancied; I remember seeing one going down the steps to Notting Hill Tube station. But a donkey would be a bother in London – especially on the Tube – and superfluous in the country, for our cottage is near a rescue centre. The mournful braying of the residents can be heard from our back garden. The centre is a depressing place: at the edge of a field is a trough at which a hundred or more formerly abused donkeys stand shoulder to shoulder, their ears waving listlessly. The management have a regular advertisement in the parish magazine, offering the opportunity to take a donkey for a half-day's walk – you mustn't ride it – at a price of twenty pounds. It seems to mean that you pay them, but it should be the other way round, for you are helping with the donkey's rehab. Presumably the route is not prescribed by the Animal Health Office.

Fluffy moved on to monkeys. She wanted a little one, which, she said, she would dress like me. On maximally fogeyish days I wear a dark-green tweed suit, a felt waistcoat, a check shirt, yellow braces and brown brogues (one of them the shoe humped by Nonsense the tortoise: it has worn well). This was the costume she envisaged for the monkey. It was a picturesque image, but I was tepid, having seen a macaque, dressed like Coco the Clown, running amok in a car at some traffic lights. I also remembered being bitten, as a child, by a marmoset that was wearing a sailor suit; dancing on top of a barrel organ, it beckoned me before sinking its teeth in – a rotten trick. Then there was the question of continence: I don't know whether you can house-train a monkey, but I doubt that you can persuade one to loosen braces, undo a buttoned fly and negotiate a pair of boxer shorts. Fluffy said that the problem would be solved with a nappy, but she was vague as to who would change it. In the end she gave up on the monkey and bought a ventriloquist's dummy which was tweedily dressed. It came from the bric-à-brac market, like the stuffed alligator that stood in for the crocodile.

Couldn't we have a more ordinary pet, I asked – a rabbit, say? Fluffy started to cry. Her mother Rosa, when a small girl, had owned a pet rabbit called Cookie. One evening Rosa's mother, an unsentimental woman of peasant stock, served rabbit stew and announced, when the family had finished, that they had just eaten Cookie. I should have remembered. Trying to cover my traces, I suggested some other sort of rodent. A rabbit isn't a rodent, Fluffy replied testily, as if that were a fact known to every schoolboy. I tried again: how about a rodent – perhaps a guinea pig? My heart was not in this suggestion, for the guinea pigs I had met were dim and timid, and looked like handleless feather dusters;

but they were less trouble than monkeys or real pigs. A young girl I knew, called Alice, kept her two guineas – Nebuchadnezzar and Belshazzar – in a bath in the corner of the kitchen; whenever I reached down to stroke either of them, it would squeak and rush into a length of pipe kept there for panic attacks. Alice's father, an architect, designed and built for the animals a beautiful hutch with pillars and finials, but Alice told him that they preferred the bath. How could she tell?

Somewhat more outgoing than Neb. and Bel. was Puffl, whom I met when visiting a lawyer called Gottfried Blank in Stuttgart. Blank, who was convinced that my name was Oliver Blank, was helping me with a merger, and one day invited me to dinner after work. His dining room had a tiled floor, and as we were eating I became aware of tiny clicking footsteps, as if made by miniature stilletos. A hazel guinea pig was teetering into the room. 'Ach, Puffl, mein Schatz!' Blank exclaimed, and for the rest of the evening I got no sense out of him. It was a relief, sense having consisted of an unsolicited lecture on Article 21(4) of the EU Merger Regulation.

Still more contemptible than guinea pigs are hamsters. My experience of these has likewise been bad. I used to lodge with a man called Gerald and his hamster Pickles, whom he spoilt in ways that Pickles didn't enjoy. Gerald had a weakness for Cadbury's Fruit and Nut, and plied the hamster with it; Pickles tactfully stored the stuff in his cheeks until his master had withdrawn, and then spat it out, littering the sawdust of his cage with brown gobbets. Gerald also had a theory that Pickles liked to be sung to; at bedtime he would lean over the cage and sing 'We Shall Overcome' in a wheezy tenor. While this was going on, Pickles would make a pile of sawdust and bury his head in it. 'He's getting ready for bye-byes' was Gerald's take. When Gerald went on holiday, I decided to liberate the hamster from his cage. Pickles scuttled about the dining room while I chased him with a woollen snake, and we were having a lovely time until he disappeared into a hole in the skirting. I had to pull up three floorboards to get him out. Before I could put him back in the cage, he whizzed up the curtains and slipped off the rail at the top. Plunging eight feet, he thumped on to the dining table, his tooth chipped, a glazed look in his eye. The vet put him out of his misery. When Gerald returned, and I gave him an edited account of the disaster, his upper lip remained stiff, but the following month he doubled the rent.

At one time I might have suggested a rat as a pet. I was attracted by one that I met on a train. A man sat down opposite me, having placed on the table between us a cage containing this large white rat with red eyes. The rat and I took a hard look at each other, before it got on to its wheel and settled down to exercise. It was lively and handsome, let down only by its revolting tail. I thought of starting a conversation with the man, but the cage got in the way, and through the two sets of bars he looked nutty and aggressive. For all I know, the rule for dogs, that you're allowed to chat to their owners, may have no counterpart for rats.

I didn't even raise the topic with Fluffy, for our house had recently been infested by wild rats. For a long time she had noticed a musky smell in her basement studio; she couldn't trace the source, and was not amused when I suggested it was she. One evening when she was working there, and I was in my study on the top floor, she called me down – by phone, for she won't be bothered with the stairs – and asked whether I could hear a noise behind one of the heaps of junk covering every square inch of the expensive parquet she had made me buy. A loud scrabbling, it was hard to miss. 'A mouse, do you think?' she asked in a quavery voice. 'A bear at least,' I replied, but it was plainly a rat. Hurriedly evacuating the cellar, we called the council. They charge for dealing with mice, but come for free if you have rats – the only bright side of the situation.

The rodent officer confirmed, by the smell and some droppings, that we had at least one rat; he traced the run to the fusebox cupboard, put down some saucers of poison there, and promised to return in a fortnight. A couple of days before his next visit, I ventured into Fluffy's lair – now only the rat's, or rats' – to check on progress. Gingerly, I opened one side of the cupboard's double doors, and was encouraged to find that some of the poison had been eaten. As I opened the other side, a portly rat sprang out at me. It was not white and glossy, like the one on the train, but brown and greasy. The cupboard being at human-eye height, the beast almost hit my face, but flew over my shoulder, and shot behind the heap from which we had first heard the scrabbling. I made a noise that can only be called a scream, and then stood there in shock. After half a minute, a nose and a pair of whiskers appeared round the edge of the heap. 'Aaaaaaaagh!' I went, and rapidly stamped my feet, Flamenco-wise. The nose and whiskers withdrew. There being a standoff, I retreated from the cellar, bolting the door behind me – a useless measure, the closed door leaving a gap generous enough for the plumpest rodent to saunter through.

The rat man came, replenished the poison, and said he would return in another fortnight. This time I forwent the prefatory inspection. On his third visit he found the poison untouched and announced that the rat or rats had left or died. With some coaxing, Fluffy resumed her chthonic routine, but a week later there was a disgusting smell in the hall, different from the musky one – more like rotting vegetables. It grew in strength and disgustingness, and clearly had something to do with the rat(s), so we again summoned the RO. 'That's a dead one,' he said cheerily. 'Must be under the floorboards.' To mask the growing stink, he left a pot of aromatic gel, which smelt almost as foul, and the two odours competed with each other over the following months. Had I known how long it would take for a rat to decompose, I would have pulled up the floorboards, as I had done for Pickles. Even now, three years later, we get the odd whiff on rainy days.

The only other rodent possible as a pet was a mouse. Say 'mouse' these days and people are likely to think of computer accessories. Harry, an old and confused friend, got into trouble on that score.

Needing a new lead for the mouse of his laptop, he went into a shop and said 'I want a longer lead for my mouse, which is left-handed.' You can see where this is going. Harry's local PC World was next to the pet shop. The assistant looking blank, Harry got impatient: 'M-O-U-S-E!' he spelt out. 'The smallest leads we have are for ferrets,' the assistant replied, pointing to a rack of them; 'I suppose one might fit a mouse.'

As in the case of rats, Fluffy and I were put off four-legged mice by the wild ones that drop in now and then; their darting across the floor is unnerving. I was running out of ideas. 'There's always a dog or a cat,' I mused. 'I hadn't thought of that,' said Fluffy.

A Tonic Cat

Wherever Fluffy and I live, most of our neighbours are gay. It's probably because we choose places ill-suited to children; the Georgian houses in our Spitalfields street have winding stairs, their floors are splintery and full of nails, and green spaces are remote. Knock on a door at random in Nell Street and the chances are that it will be answered by a gay man clasping a cat. Just to take our side of the road: At number two lives Miles, who has a Siamese called Ricky. Miles, a noisy man, shouts in Ricky's face, and the cat gazes pityingly back at him. Little more than a kitten, Ricky won't be deaf, unlike poor Mungo, the eighteen-year-old ginger who lives at number four with Tony and Ian. Unable to hear himself miaow, Mungo does so fortissimo; you get a fright if he starts up behind you. Jack Ashley, after losing his hearing, would get a colleague to signal to him if he was speaking too loudly or too softly in the House of Commons, but Tony and Ian fail to provide Mungo

125

with a similar service. They are insensitive to the feelings of an old chap: dotted around the house are his predecessors, stuffed, and Ian talked of turning Mungo into a stole when his turn came – a rotten idea, given the state of the cat's coat. Eventually the fur became so matted that Tony, an anaesthetist, knocked Mungo out, and Ian, a hairdresser, shaved all of him except the head, tail and paws. Mungo's broad smiling face was far too large for his skinny torso, and he looked as if he was wearing football boots.

We are at number six, at number eight is another straight couple, and next to them is Leo, a camp person. 'I've handed in my notice,' he confided to me; 'they're homophobic where I work.' I asked him his line of business. 'Power tools,' he replied. 'Ooooooh, they're awfully homophobic in power tools.' It is a shame they are no longer making *Carry On* films. Leo has three cats, each a different obscure breed. One is naked (it doesn't even wear boots), the second has wool instead of fur, and the third has the ears of a bat. When we were introduced, I had to convert a gasp of horror into one of admiration. Leo keeps them indoors, the house is dark, and so the three freaks are highly strung; they prowl around, moaning contralto discords.

Foolishly, I agreed to feed them when Leo went on a week's holiday. The instructions he left were baroque: each cat had its own diet, the woolly one had a syrup for constipation, and they ate at different times from each other. I was running back and forth and, when I tried to give any one its private meal, the others would barge in and start gobbling. By day three my patience had run out, and from then on I fed them all at the same times, on a mixture of their diets, with a few drops of the syrup on top. It seemed not to do them any harm. I should have simply stopped feeding them, for they are all obese and on their way to coronaries. If Leo asks me to look after his cats again, I shall refuse, and he will have to rely on Marjorie, the local animal-minder, who will feed your cat for five pounds a day – whether per cat or per house, I don't know, but in either case it's stiff, given the time it takes to put out a bowl of muck. Marjorie claims that she also plays with the cat, but I imagine the cat usually absolves her from that duty: they have to be in the mood.

Beyond Leo, at number twelve, is Cedric, who used to have a splendid grey neutered tom called Esau. This cat was known as the King of Nell Street: in the evenings he would stroll up and down the pavement, rubbing against the legs of passers-by and graciously receiving their homage. Because Cedric, an investment banker, would get home late, Esau used to drop into our house, giving us all the pleasure of possessing a cat and none of the burdens. Cedric, who had the burdens without the pleasure, disliked the arrangement, but we denied that it existed, and there was not much he could do about it. Except on special occasions, we did not feed Esau, and he was content to enjoy our company. A routine developed: he would sit under a car at the end of the street and, when I came round the corner on my way back from the office, he would emerge, trot down the pavement beside me, sit on the doorstep while I unlocked the door, and then rush in. His movements were accompanied by the ringing of a heavy bell attached to his collar, as if he were a leper. In the belief that the ringing got on his nerves, Fluffy squirted Super Glue into the bell to jam the clapper. That night Esau padded off in silence, but the following evening the bell was ringing again. The process was repeated four times before Fluffy gave up. Does Super Glue not work on bells? Did Cedric unpick the glue each time? Both hypotheses are far-fetched.

After supper, Esau and I would go upstairs to the sitting room, to listen to music. Once the disc was on, I would kneel on the floor and comb him, for Esau was an hairy cat: I worried that he would get fur balls (absent any others). The combing over, I would sit on the sofa with Esau on my knee, where sometimes he would fall asleep and sometimes become horny. On horny evenings he would knead my thighs while staring into my eyes with a faraway look; then a tiny purple knob would appear, and his haunches would quiver. Once he ejaculated – to my surprise, given his lack of testicles, but perhaps the fluid is produced elsewhere: I'm hazy about these things. 'Ooh, Esau!' I tittered. Moppet, the neutered tom I grew up with, used to carry on in the same way: my mother had trouble with him when she was wearing a mohair jersey, and he couldn't resist humping the feather duster, although it embarrassed him to be seen doing so.

One evening, while Esau was on the job, there was a knock on the front door. I shut him in the sitting room and went downstairs. On the doorstep was Cedric, who had come, as Spitalfields fogeys often do, with a petition to sign against a building development in the area. While we were chatting in the doorway, I saw, from the corner of my eye, Esau coming round the bend of the stairs, lured by HMV. I had not shut him in properly. Cedric, facing the staircase, must have seen him too; but, just in case he hadn't, I moved forward over the threshold, pulling the front door to behind me. The manoeuvre pressed my chest against Cedric's and forced him down a step. The conversation over, we said a gentlemanly goodnight as if nothing had happened, but there had been plenty of I-know-that-he-knows-that-I-think... It was like *The Golden Bowl*.

Esau grew old and bony. I told Fluffy that if he died I would kill myself, and she tactlessly passed this on to Cedric, who affected bafflement. He said that Esau was off his tucker, but I suspected that the problem was a combination of hard food and rotten teeth – Esau had a gold filling – and so, when Esau next visited, we unwontedly gave him a bowl of mince, which he hoovered up. I felt again the guilt that had overwhelmed me when my mother and I took Moppet, then very doddery, to the vet and my mother asked 'Has he lost a tooth?' The vet replied 'Let's put it this way: he has *got* a tooth.' I claimed to love Moppet – when small I had thumped a schoolfriend for attaching a sticky label to his nose – but negligence had caused me to let him suffer agonies while his teeth dropped out one by one. By that time Moppet was as deaf as Mungo, and slept even more than cats usually do, changing position and location only once or twice a day. A heartless friend said that he had been dead for years, and that we moved him around the flat to create a simulacrum of life, as the Yugoslavs had done, *mutatis mutandis*, with President Tito.

Cedric claimed not to be sentimental about pets, and normally would not let a cat into the bedroom, but one evening, when Esau seemed strangely melancholy, Cedric lifted him on to the bed (he was too frail to jump). During the night, when Cedric turned over, he heard a thud on the floor: it was Esau's corpse, which had rolled off. Cedric's profession of apatheia was belied by his tenderly wrapping the body in a cashmere cardigan borrowed from some other old queen in the street – Leo, I think. He then put the package in the fridge, pending Esau's burial under a flagstone in the back yard. The cleaning lady, putting milk away, was startled to find a cardigan in the fridge, and more so to catch Esau's now glassy eye peering out of the cardigan. Esau is survived by Cedric's other cat, Becky – a silly, candy-flossy thing, also old, but much sprightlier since Esau's death. They hated each other.

As Esau approached his end, and Fluffy and I began to dread the vacuum he would leave, we decided to get a cat of our own. Miles had bought Ricky from Paws Rescue Centre, which he recommended: they have a website, with photos and cloying descriptions of the current residents. We were attracted by a little black one, which we made an appointment to see. In

the flesh it was cringeing and mangey, so we asked
Dot, the girl on duty, to show us some others. A
majestic grey tom, who reminded me of Esau in his
prime, was purring at the front of his cage. 'Tell me
about him,' I said to Dot. 'Lovely, isn't he,' she
replied; 'he's diabetic – you need to give him an
injection twice a day.' We walked on.

At the back of each cage was a box with a hole,
for the cat to retire into if it wanted privacy. Poking
out of one hole was the front end of a pretty tabby.
The label on the cage said 'Suki – three years old'. I
am fond of tabbies: Moppet was one, and a
psychologist I know told me that their average IQ is
two points higher than that of other cats. I don't
know how they measure it. Dot opened the cage,
Suki revealed more of herself, and when we stroked
her she started to purr. 'This is the one,' I declared.
As Suki needed vaccinations, we could not take her
with us, but we paid a deposit. Driving home, it
dawned on me that we had not seen her back half:
perhaps she was a Manx, perhaps her hind legs were
paralysed, perhaps she had no hind legs but wheels
instead, like the dog in a photo I once saw. (Peeing
against a lamp post must have been hard.) Fluffy
turned the car round, and we went back for a 360-
degree examination of Suki, who, now at the front of
the cage, proved to be intact. 'She's very placid,' Dot
said, lifting her out. 'You can tip her any way you
like.' The cat was then rotated through various
angles, and didn't protest. 'She's the darling of the
cattery,' Dot prattled on. The title was no doubt
bestowed on every cat in front of its prospective

owner. I asked why Suki had been handed in. 'Owner said he found he was allergic to cats. It's a common excuse. If that many people were allergic to them, the whole population would be sneezing.' Fluffy sneezed.

In the days between introduction and collection, Fluffy and I pondered new names for the cat: 'Suki' was soppy (and 'Fluffy' too late to change). Agreeing that an old-fashioned name would be best, we found on the web a list of Victorian girls' names, and lit on 'Maud'. The disadvantage was that the cat's name would be less catty than my wife's, but Fluffy refused to swap. The advantage was that 'Maud' was short, and answerable-to by an animal, and had happy associations for me: my parents used to have a cleaner called Maud Snusher, who was so kindhearted that she let me ride on her back while she was scrubbing the floor. I was thirty-five at the time (just joking).

The new Maud, although nervous when we brought her home, caught a mouse on her first evening. Our house, riddled with cracks and holes, had until then been a murine playground, but Maud has instituted a disciplinarian regime, glaring sternly for hours at the skirting in the hope of pouncing on miscreants. We call it watching Mouse Telly. When she tires of that, she enjoys Bird Radio, which involves sitting on the large radio by our kitchen window and watching the birds in the back yard. When one of them hops on to the sill, and there are only a couple of inches and a pane of glass between Maud and it, Maud chatters and her whiskers dance. I was familiar with this behaviour from my mother's

132

cat Thisbe, whom I used to torment with a portable typewriter.[1] Thisbe was fascinated by the way the typewriter's letters rose on their stalks: if I pressed a key gently, causing the stalk to rise, she would tap the end of it gingerly, as if it might give her an electric shock. I would then press another key, and she would jump as a different stalk began to rise. If I carried on long enough, she would chatter and twitch her whiskers, and sometimes got so carried away that she gagged. I would end the session by pressing the carriage release: the carriage shot sideways, a bell rang, and Thisbe leapt vertically from all paws before tearing off.

Sometimes, when Maud was sitting on the radio, she turned it on by pressing a button with her bottom. If it was on already, she would change the channel. We therefore covered the buttons with a large cookery book, and Maud now sits on the face of Delia. If Maud wants to look from the front of the house, she goes into the dining room, the windows of which give directly on to the street; like an old lady behind net curtains, she enjoys watching the commuters going one way in the morning, the other way in the evening. To give her a commanding view, Fluffy has supplied a stand specially designed for cats; it was rotting in the garden of a client whose house Fluffy was redecorating, so she asked him whether she could take it home. He agreed without consulting his wife or cat, who both looked sourly on

---

[1] When clearing out the flat after my mother died, Fluffy threw this lovely machine away, along with a valuable pre-Columbian figurine which she took to be a knick-knack won at a fairground.

as Fluffy dragged it to the car. The structure, covered in shaggy nylon, is a cross between a cakestand and a crazy-golf obstacle, with three platforms joined by ladders, steps and slopes. There is a touch of Gaudi about it, and it clashes with our Georgian interior. Maud has no time for the gimmicks, but likes to roost on the top platform, about five feet high, which she reaches in one leap, causing the stand to sway alarmingly.

As advised by an RSPCA fact sheet, we have tried to entertain her with toys, but she has little time for them. There is a plastic stick with feathers on the end, which we wave in front of her; now and then she will lunge at it, but she finds the encounter overwhelming and soon retires under a chair, where she unwinds with a large catnip cigar. When she is ready for her daytime nap, which lasts ten hours, I carry her to my study, and she snores or whistles beside me while I work, occasionally waking herself up from a dream with a miaow. We are like Jerome and the lion.

When Maud joined the family, Esau, just about alive, would still turn up for his nightly visits. Darting through the front door as usual, he came face to face with Maud, who took a dim view of the intrusion. Poor Esau sat nonplussed in the face of Maud's hissing and growling, and we had to put him out on the front step, where he was still sitting an hour later, hoping that we would all see sense. Fluffy and I had betrayed him. We felt terrible.

Spitalfields being gritty even in its most genteel parts, we had intended to keep Maud indoors, but she looked so wistful, gazing out of the window, that we decided to let her into the yard, which has high walls, like the exercise ground of a prison, allowing her to take the air but not to break out – or so we thought until a giant leap at a bird propelled her to the top of a wall. Resigning ourselves to her being an outdoor cat, we installed a puss flap and, to avoid her breaking a leg with another such jump, propped a ladder against the wall.

Her excursions relieve the strain on her lavatory, which is in an alcove between the kitchen and the back door. I eat my breakfast at that end of the kitchen, and Maud times her morning dump to coincide with my Alpen. Her dry food looks similar to muesli. On the sack the pellets are described as 'kibbles', but I think 'kibble' is a mass noun like 'rubble', not a count noun like 'pebble': the plural is a translating howler, the food being made in France. It's as bad as the translation on the box of some French stuff my father bought to get rid of moles in the garden: 'Struggle against moles!' it said. The kibble(s) produce(s) mercifully hard stools, but they are richly aromatic, as Waitrose says of its French Blend coffee, with which I accompany the Alpen.

The litter tray is in a small house, with a door that swings from a hinge at the top. When Maud paws the litter, which comes in a sack saying 'As Used in Abattoirs', it sounds like a Mexican vigorously playing the maracas; when she scrapes it with her back legs, knocking the door as she does so, the door swings violently as if by itself. It's not as bad as the craps of Titus, another cat of my mother's, who used to expel man-sized turds into the flower box just outside the dining-room window when we were eating lunch. My mother would hunt for them under the geraniums, as if they were free-range eggs, and pick them up with a spoon and fork.

Maud probably shits in number eight's garden, and I worry that the neighbours might take revenge with an airgun, or with some broken glass in a titbit. In any event, the decision to let her out is one for which we have paid – Maud figuratively, Oliver literally. A week or so after her jump to freedom, she was chased to the threshold of her own flap by an angry tom. Recognising that such encounters are likely to be more frequent and violent at night, we entice her indoors at bed time by shaking the kibble sack at the back door. Once she is in, we try to remember to drop the flap's portcullis – a sliding plastic partition. If, as usually happens, our minds wander, she shoots out again and disappears over the garden wall. She is too cunning to be lured by a second shaking of the sack.

One night she failed to appear. The following morning I found her in the basement area at the front: she had gone round the block and found our house. She had trouble jumping out and was clearly lame, so we drove her to Mr Bobal, the vet. Things had got off to a bad start with Bobal when we had taken Maud to him for a check-up and he had said that she was shabby. 'What do you mean, shabby!' Fluffy cried. 'She has a lovely glossy coat – Oliver combs her every day.' 'No, no, *shabby*, the cat is *shabby*,' Bobal insisted. Blows were about to be exchanged when we realised that his Czech accent was leading us astray: he meant 'chubby', and that we were feeding her too much. That was still upsetting, given the care I take to measure out her kibble – which I precede, by way of *amuse-bouche*, with a teaspoonful of pâté made for cats but yummy enough for humans (I dipped my finger in it).

When we took Maud in with her gammy leg, Bobal plonked her on the floor and watched her hobble around the surgery. There was a wound in her thigh, which he attributed to another cat, or to a rat, a dog or a fox.[2] He told us to leave Maud with him and to collect her in the evening. When we returned, he had shaved her leg and stitched it. He had also, he said, given her a CAT scan and a PET scan. No doubt, if she had been a Labrador, there would have been a lab report. The bill was £1,400. Too late, I resolved to take out pet insurance. The price included some painkiller, which Bobal told us to squirt into Maud's mouth with a syringe four times a day. This proved hard, Maud clamping her teeth together and shaking her head, so that more of the stuff went on to us than into her.

The next morning there were patches of vomit all over the kitchen floor. Maud, huddled in the corner, was listless and obviously very ill, so we took her back

[2] Foxes are ten-a-penny in Nell Street: they come over from the disused sidings outside Liverpool Street station and rip open the sacks of rubbish. Hunting should be allowed in Spitalfields. Fluffy, when she finds them at it, chases them down the street, waving her arms like windmill sails and emitting whooping noises. In the area round our country cottage they are rarer; I was excited when, as I thought, I glimpsed one, but it turned out to be a ginger cat.

to Bobal. As we lifted her out of the car in her flimsy box, its handle fell off and she fell into the road. I decided that Fluffy and I could not be trusted with a pet. Bobal, puzzled, told us that he would have to take Maud as an in-patient in his 'hospital' – a few cages in a basement under the surgery. Mindful of the £1,400, I had a difficult conversation with Fluffy in the car on the way home: how much were we willing to pay for further treatment? I proposed ten thousand, Fluffy twenty – but then it was not her money. We chose not to think of the number of blind African children whose eyesight could be restored with such a sum.

During Maud's week in hospital, we visited every day. Maud was on a drip, and very feeble, but when she saw us arrive she would totter to the front of her cage. We would open the door and alternately rest our brows against hers, weeping freely. Fluffy asked Bobal whether Maud was likely to die. 'I am not thinking so bad yet,' he replied, but looked grave. He went on to speculate that her illness might have been caused by the painkiller: several of his other patients had shown the same reaction. We had managed to squirt enough in her gob to bring her to death's door, even if not to relieve her pain. Fluffy – astute despite her anguish – pounced on his guileless revelation: if Bobal had caused the illness, he should take that fact into account when charging for the cure. A granitic negotiator, she got him down to forty-five pounds for the whole stay, including drugs.

Maud recovered, and her only health problem since has been car sickness in journeys to and from our cottage in Dorset. I tried driving prophylactically slowly, to the rage of other road users, but it didn't work: one evening, when we were trundling along at twenty miles an hour, with even a tractor in the queue behind us, Maud not only chucked, but defecated for good measure. Bobal prescribed pills, which he said were licensed only for dogs but worked for cats too; perhaps because of the pasting Fluffy had given him over the fee, he made me sign a disclaimer acknowledging the limits of regulatory approval. The pills do the trick, but are no easier than the poisonous painkiller to get into Maud. At first Fluffy and I tried a double act: I knelt behind Maud, pressed her between my knees, and wrenched open her jaws; Fluffy inserted the pill, I clamped the jaws, and Fluffy stroked Maud's neck until we could assume that the pill had gone down. Maud made as if to swallow, and then, once we had released her, blew the pill out, like an Amazonian with a poisoned dart. Now, therefore, I grind the pill up and hide it in her pâté; but, no matter how fine the powder, she manages to eat round most of it. She has only herself to blame if she feels queer.

If she had the capacity, she would judge that the car journeys were worthwhile, for she is happier in Dorset than in London. The cottage has a back garden, into which Maud comes, and there she pounces on the mice and shrews that emerge from the compost heap. As cats do, she likes to bring them indoors, announcing the delivery with a proud miaow. Often the poor little thing is alive, and I have to judge whether to attempt a rescue or to let nature take its course. When I was brushing my teeth before bed, Maud brought in a shrew which ran over my bare foot as she chased it round the bathroom floor. The creature was limping, so I decided that, if Maud did not finish the job soon, I would have to put it out of its misery. Finding a hammer, and reckless of possible cracks to the tiles, I joined Maud in the chase, which ended when I inadvertently trod on the shrew. It burst under my heel. I found it hard to get to sleep, and when I did so I had sanguinary dreams.

It is a relief that she only chatters and twitches at birds, and fails to catch them. Moppet used to bring in fluttering ones, including a yellowhammer which scattered its gaudy feathers around the sitting room. Maud has also not yet taken on a rabbit. Moppet would shun these – when, in old age, he bumped into one in the garden, he averted his gaze and hurried on – but I have seen Titus, of the large stools, eat a rabbit, almost as large as he was, in one sitting: he started with the ears, while the thing was alive and screaming, and left only a small green organ – the spleen, possibly. For the next three days he was comatose, like a python after eating a pig.

On the rare occasions when you want Maud to catch an animal, she shows no interest. There's an outfit called The Curtain Exchange, where refined old ladies sell you curtains, with years of wear left in them, that have been cast off by the affluent. The ones we bought there for the cottage's sitting room were inhabited by a large mouse – a borderline rat – which lay low till they were hung, but it then started to zoom up and down the folds while I was writing at the table by the window. As Maud was stretched out with her tail listlessly brushing my keyboard, I pulled her upright and manhandled her head so that it was pointing at the curtain in question. 'Look, Maud: MOUSE. Do something!' I urged. She cast a bored glance at the curtain, then jumped off the table and went upstairs to bed, so I started banging the folds with a walking stick. The mouse retired to the lining. Only a few days later did Maud get down to business: finding her swinging from the top of the curtain by her front paws, I was worried that she would pull down the rail, which was screwed to crumbling plaster. The Tarzan act was no more effective than the walking-stick routine, but the following morning I found the mouse lying dead. You have to let cats take their time.

Dead mice in the morning are a hazard. Maud likes to eat the back end, so I am often greeted by one or two mouse heads, sometimes plus bust, peering up from the rug. The pattern makes them hard to discern, so it's a Where's Wally situation; I pick my way cautiously to the kitchen, in order to avoid more goo on the underside of my foot. A neighbour tells me that his cat likes the front end of the mouse: perhaps the two cats could come to an arrangement.

I wish we had got a cat sooner: had we done so, there would have been more joy in our lives. I drone on about Maud to bored friends and indulgent readers; when she's not there, I smile if I think of her; and when she is there I speak to her in a soppy falsetto. It used to annoy me when people nattered to their pets, but I can no longer throw stones. I would be mortified to hear a recording of the things I say to Maud: 'You're Daddy's little bubsy, aren't you, darling,' and similar. When she is asleep or drowsy, I comb whichever side of her is exposed, and, so as not to disturb her, go back later to comb the other side when she has turned over. 'Daddy has done your lefty, hasn't he, sweetheart,' I murmur; 'now he's going to do your righty. Mmmmmm, that's lovely, isn't it, tumsy?'

Fluffy, when she hears me carrying on like this, says 'You love Maud more than you love me.' '*Of course* I do,' I reply. Maud doesn't argue, have bad moods, tell fibs, leave her shoes lying around, 'borrow' money, or invite ghastly people into the house. I also remind Fluffy that in pre-Maud days, when we were humming and hahing about getting a cat, she would say, as an argument in favour, 'I want something to love.' But there is love and love. I am fonder of Maud than I am of Fluffy, but I am more deeply attached to the latter than to the former. The test is one of fungibility: whatever Clemenceau may have said about cemeteries, Fluffy would be hard to replace, but if Maud were run over I would soon find another little angel, of whom I would be just as fond.

I am not belittling the grief a cat's death can cause, even though you are setting yourself up for it by getting a pet with such a short span. (It's different if you are terminally ill or buy a tortoise.) My mother had a hard time of it when Titus got cancer of the spine. First he started missing the target when jumping on to things, then his gait became jerky, and then he started to drag his back legs. When he was barely able to walk, my mother decided that he should be put down. She wanted it done at home, she said, and I would have to be there. I was busy at the time, but I dashed over to her flat between meetings. The vet explained that he would inject into Titus's paw a drug that would kill him instantly and painlessly. When my mother said that she wanted him to do it while Titus was on her lap, the vet warned that Titus would pee on her trousers. 'I don't mind,' she said, shaking her head and holding back tears. Titus, sensing that something was up, dragged himself under a chair, and I had to scoop him out. Tearful myself now, I put him on my mother's knee, and she stroked him until he had settled down. The drug went into the paw, the cat went floppy, the pee went into the trousers. That was it. 'They used this a lot during the war,' the vet said, in a lame attempt at conversation. Presumably he was not talking about pets; I didn't like to ask, but I observed that this drug gave them a happier release than many humans were allowed by their doctors, and I asked where you could buy the stuff. Hurriedly changing the subject, he produced a folder of photos showing a weed-infested field, in which he said we could have Titus buried; but the price was ridiculous, and so we settled for incineration. The vet slid the body into a blue plastic bag, took his cheque, and off he went. Thisbe, the typist, had looked on throughout, unmoved, from the mantelpiece. She stood to Titus as Becky did to Esau, and was no friendlier to Lofty, Titus's replacement. Lofty was a dwarf – not rare in breed, but stunted in limbs and tail: he looked like a walking tea cosy. After a couple of years, he too succumbed to cancer.

It is said to be a vice of the English that they lavish more love on animals than on people. My mother had harsh words for Mrs Slowcock, my piano teacher, who drooled over her own cat: it was because she hated Mr Slowcock and her children had left home, my mother said. Such judgments can fail to distinguish the kinds of love. Mrs S may have hated Mr S, but she may have loved him and the cat in different ways, as I do Maud and Fluffy. Even if she loved them in the same way, and even if she loved the cat more than Mr S, there may have been plenty of love to go round. I am not convinced that the alleged vice of the English is a vice.

You may say that my love of Maud rests on an illusion that she loves me back, one caused by projecting my feelings on to her. Maud's curling up on my knee, the charge runs, means only that she is comfortable; in so far as she feels warmly towards me, it is because I am the gateway to dinner. My reply is threefold. First, the charge underestimates the capacity cats have for affection. Thisbe was so devoted to me that, when I packed a suitcase to go away, she vomited into it. Second, it also applies to love between humans, which – you don't need Proust to tell you – is often based on projection and illusion. Third, I don't care whether Maud loves me or not: I love her anyway. Of course my love involves wilful blindness – in particular, to the hecatombs of mice and shrews, and of the cows and pigs that are turned into kibble. Is that worse than buying for your privileged children clothes that are made by deprived children?

I am more troubled by the sadistic fantasies that are woven into my love for Maud. For large tea parties, Fluffy and I have an urn, of which I am proud. Often, when the water in it is boiling, I picture myself snatching Maud up, throwing her in, and putting the lid on. Once, when the urn was on and she was walking past, I realised that I was eyeing her fiendishly. It doesn't amount to an intention, but it's more than an idle image, and there is something pleasurable about it. My friend Moses reports that he has a similar fantasy about sawing his chihuahua in half. It's odd, given our love for these animals – but love has many guises.

A Guide to Dogs

Seneca gives examples of the annoyances that a Stoic sage should rise above. One is: a dog hanging around. It's a piquant glimpse of the man, and it endears him to me. You are said to be either a dog person or a cat person: *tertium datur*, no doubt, but in any event I am not a dog person. True, a cat, like a dog, may hang around, but it will not look gormless while doing so, it does not need to be taken for walks, and you can choose your time to shovel its shit, rather than fawningly pursuing it along the pavement with a small plastic bag.

With a dog, most of the fawning is in the other direction. When I visited Herbert Barth, an antiquarian bookseller in Tübingen, his Doberman, Fester, greeted me by putting his front legs on my chest and licking my face. We had not met before. As I tried to break free, Barth and his wife stood there chortling. They were just as insouciant and merry when Fester wrapped his legs around the neck of their two-year-old daughter Claudia, and started humping her from behind. I could see his evil pink sausage. We were having lunch beside their swimming pool, and Claudia had been toddling around; once Fester had her in his grip, his convulsive jerks caused her to stagger towards the edge of the deep end. Only when she was a metre away did Mrs Barth intervene. If Claudia had been pushed in, she would not have drowned, but would have been concussed, for the pool contained no water: Barth stored his books in it, the straight shelves squeezing awkwardly against the kidney-shaped walls. It was a Swimming Pool Library. Claudia found Fester's attentions as funny as her parents did: she commented delightedly in perfect German word order, stacking her participles up at the end of her sentences. That impressed me, for I had just begun learning the language. In preparation for the visit, I had worked up an elaborate German sentence along the lines of 'I'm afraid you may find that I am not as conversant with the finer points of vocabulary and syntax as you might have expected from our previous correspondence.' When I reeled this off, Barth exclaimed, *auf deutsch*, 'But your German is excellent!' Thereafter he and his wife prattled away to me incomprehensibly, and I responded with nods and smiles.

Fawning of a less carnal kind was the speciality of Winkle, the King Charles bitch owned by my friend Dan – or, to be more accurate, foisted upon the household by his wife Amelia. Winkle would gawp up at you with her bluebottle eyes; each was the size and colour of her nose, and the three together looked like a socket for a giant three-pin plug. I longed to insert one and to administer a death-dealing current. She was too wet to bark. When she and Dan were alone in the flat, a burglar climbed through the window of the sitting room and stole the bibelots. Dan could be excused for not noticing, as he was in his study, busy with philosophy. Winkle, who was reclining on the sitting-room sofa throughout, failed to alert him, and no doubt treated the burglar to one of her vacant stares.

The breeds vary in intelligence, King Charles spaniels being near the bottom of the ladder. The IQ of a mongrel is harder to predict. Rex – the quarter-beagle, quarter-boxer, quarter-whippet, quarter-God-knows – belonging to the family of Benjy Warnick, a friend at prep school, was both dim and uncouth. When I was staying with the Warnicks, and Benjy and I had gone to bed, Rex settled on my chest, his bottom in my face, and let out a vile fart of digested Chum. I heaved him off, causing Benjy to accuse me of cruelty to animals. A fight ensued. I say that Benjy was my friend, but I despised him: he was a weed and had a stutter, and it delighted me that my parents were much richer than his. The Warnicks lived in a cramped flat, from which Rex bolted whenever the opportunity arose. Phone calls on the topic were frequent – to the police ('Have you found our dog?') and from the local butcher ('I've got your dog, and he's stolen another string of sausages'). Rex was an ace at stealing food. One evening he polished off a large and unattended ham in the kitchen, and the next morning his turds were streaked with red. The Warnicks worried that the vast meal had ruptured his insides, but closer inspection revealed that the streaks were bits of the red string that had tied the ham. Rex didn't restrict himself to meat: on the day of the reappearing string, half a Victoria sponge went the way of the ham. Benjy's mother, Jane, tidied up the remaining half, smoothing off the tooth marks, and served it for tea.

Rex's most daring escape was not from the flat but from the Warnicks' Ford Cortina. We were driving to the Chilterns for a picnic lunch and, as we were bowling along a busy dual carriageway at fifty miles an hour, he leapt from the window. There was uproar. Warnick *père* turned back at the next roundabout, and we drove slowly along in search of the corpse. To the family's joy, but not mine, we spotted Rex licking his testicles on the central reservation: he looked bemused – he always did – but was unharmed. Darting through the traffic to rescue him was riskier than the jump that had landed him there.

After this drama, Rex's appetite was even keener than usual: as we ate our picnic, he stalked around, waiting to catch one of us off guard. So far as I was concerned, he could help himself: Jane had produced spam, cold baked beans, grey hardboiled eggs, and undressed lettuce, the leaves of which were flabby, gritty, and thick enough to pass for cabbage. Even Rex drew the line at this, and settled for peeing on my lunch. I yelled. 'Oh, don't make such a fuss,' said Jane, whose father had been in the army. 'Push the bit Rex has peed on to the side of the plate, and eat the rest.' It fitted with her repair of the Victoria sponge, and might have been the right attitude when on manoeuvres, but it struck me as unduly spartan for a picnic, so I replied that Rex had peed on everything. It was more or less true: the lettuce leaf had borne the brunt, and now sagged under a puddle of canine vinaigrette, but there were spots of pee elsewhere. I could see one glistening on the horrible spam.

More intelligent than the likes of Winkle and Rex are corgis, who, despite their ugliness, have the royal blessing; when my father went to lunch at Buckingham Palace, the Queen was preceded into the room by four of the dogs.[1] I have seen the product of crossing a corgi with a Labrador. The only corgiish component was the legs: when the dog was sitting, it looked like an ordinary Lab; when it was standing, it was grotesquely low-slung; and, when it moved from sitting to standing, the angle of its back barely changed.

Stretch a small corgi and you get a dachshund, which is yet higher up the intelligence ladder. I know a woman who uses a live one as a stole: it

---

[1] The only other noteworthy fact from my father's report of the occasion was that at the Palace they remove your plate as soon as you have finished, whether or not others are still eating. Paul Scofield – another guest and a slow eater – was still working on his potatoes when everyone else was staring at an empty mat. My mother, when she heard this, said it was 'ignorant' to clear away before everyone had finished. She also said it was 'vulgar' to cut lettuce, rather than tear it, and she took a dim view of the Queen's cutting some iceberg – itself vulgar, per my mother – in that fly-on-the-wall documentary about the royal family. At least Her Majesty didn't dump a whole leaf on your plate, as Jane Warnick had done at the picnic; nor did the corgis piss on it.

doesn't seem to mind, and it goes to a lot of parties in that capacity. As a child my mother had a share in a rough-haired dachshund called Richard. Which part of the dog had she owned, I asked when I was little, and she explained that it had been a time share. Richard was bright enough to notice when a bath was being prepared for him: hating baths, he would retreat under the bed and growl if anyone approached. His memory was short, however, and he was keener on going for walks than on avoiding baths; so, when the water was ready, my grandfather Septimus, brighter still than Richard, would put on his hat and coat, walk to the front door and call 'Richard, walkies!' Richard, bounding up, was whisked into the bath before he could say Jack Robinson.[2]

Dachshunds look sweet, but I am told that because of their length they have back trouble, which can cause their tummies to scrape the ground – a condition that might, I suppose, be relieved with a caster. It is wrong to breed dogs into disability. Pugs have such flat faces that they can't breathe properly. Clare, a neighbour of ours, has a specimen called

---

[2] Septimus was accomplished at deceiving people as well as dogs. He looked rather like George VI and, when during that monarch's reign he was going to a funeral in a large black Daimler, he took it into his head to wave at passers-by. 'The King, the King!' they cried – unlikely as it was, for they were in the rougher end of Birkenhead. His phone number was similar to that of the local cinema; fed up with people calling to ask what was on, he would make up programmes and times. 'Is there a Mickey Mouse?' a caller asked. 'No, tonight it's Donald Duck,' Septimus replied. I don't know why he was called Septimus, for he was an only child. So was my mother, and so am I: we are a rare breed.

Snuffles, who not only breathes in the way his name suggests, but also, judging by his goose-step, lacks knees. The first time Clare brought him to our house, I mistook him for a small black cat and bent down to stroke him – recoiling when I caught his batlike phiz, his bellows-to-mend respiration, and his rotting-corpse stink. Hieronymus Bosch would have had nightmares.

Inflate a pug and you get a bulldog. The bitch of the breed, I learn, has been bred into such deformity that she cannot give birth unaided. Why would anyone increase the population by lending aid? There is a bullbitch, called Grace, at our local garage. Like Snuffles, Grace pongs and can neither breathe nor walk; she spends the day propped against a petrol pump, on which she occasionally rubs her warty neck. You could sometimes glimpse a collar in the neck's fatty folds, but this has been replaced by a harness which looks like a pair of Y-fronts worn on the wrong pair of limbs. In winter Grace wears a Victorian man's bathing suit, striped, with short sleeves front and back.

The most intelligent breed I know is the poodle. I used to think that poodles were an embarrassment, but my mind was changed by Igor, a miniature – one size up from a toy – belonging to my friend Kate. They go well together, for Kate, like Igor, is black, with curly hair and a long face.[3] As dogs go, Igor has many virtues: as well as being clever, he is affectionate

---

[3] I once saw a Rastafarian with a matching poodle, the dog's coat having been tied in dreadlocks.

and doesn't smell, bark, or shed hair. He also enjoys being sung to. When Kate urged me to give Igor a song, I was shy, but she coaxed me into a rendition of 'For Sentimental Reasons' – an old Mildred Bailey number. While I warbled away, Igor sat at my feet and gazed up, spellbound. A recitalist at Wigmore Hall could wish for such an attentive and considerate audience: Igor didn't cough, rustle a programme, unwrap a sweet, or make his hearing aid whistle. He was clearly keen on Mildred, so I followed on – inhibition cast to the winds – with 'Someday Sweetheart', 'Ol' Pappy' and 'I'd Love to Take Orders From You'. He wagged his tail to the lines:

> I know that rules were made for fools,
> That's one thing I have learned.
> But I'm going in for discipline
> Wherever you're concerned.

On the debit side, Igor is a bit of a sissy. When he, Kate and I went for a walk in the country, Kate asked me to hold his lead while she went for a pee. As soon as she had gone behind a bush, Igor started to quiver and whimper. Kate was not even out of sight: her head was visible above the bush, and her feet below – as with the doors of some American public lavatories. I am also irritated by Kate's constant nattering to Igor, but I can't blame the dog for that – and I no longer blame Kate, for now I drone on to my cat Maud in the same way.

I have even come round to the bizarre hair-dos to which poodles are subjected – the most elaborate being the Continental clip, which pollards the animal and reduces its tail to a cauliflower floret. There used to be a dogs' hairdresser called Fido Sassoon, which specialised in such things and would dye your poodle the colour of your choice. I recently saw a medium poodle sporting the coiffure: his coat – newly washed, dyed and blow-dried – was a pale lilac and as puffy as a cumulus cloud, and there were pink ribbons around his neck and ears. He looked like Liberace.

Standard poodles – the big ones – are serious dogs. I encountered one when I was walking in Hyde Park with my friend Bella and her chihuahua Megan – a peevish, yapping creature. Bella has an exalted job and a chauffeur, whom she details to drive to her house at lunchtime in order to entertain Megan; at first he objected that it was outside his duties, but you don't argue with Bella. In the park, Megan cut up rough when a standard poodle bent down to sniff her privates. The poodle, huffy in turn, grabbed Megan in its jaws and started shaking her, causing both Megan and Bella to shriek. There was no sign of the poodle's owner, but a good, nay officious, Samaritan, who was jogging past, intervened by hammering as hard as he could on the poodle's head. As this was covered in wool, the blows had no effect – other than, possibly, to lodge the dog's teeth more deeply in Megan – so the man then inserted his fingers in the poodle's nostrils, causing it to drop Megan in the interest of drawing breath. It was a brave and inspired stroke, but its result was that Megan and Bella rounded on him. Maybe they mistook him for the poodle's owner; maybe panic had clouded their reason. He jogged off in disgust.

If you are a large dog, it's child's play to seize a chihuahua in your chops. A Rottweiler I know, called Horace, will seize a large branch at one end, his owner Sue takes the other end, and Horace swings Sue from one side of the garden to the other, just by shaking his head. Sue is a big girl. Horace displays affection by running up to you and slobbering in your crotch, and Sue will drawl 'Oh Horace, do stop it' – whereupon he will slink under a table and make some puffing noises to himself. They are an odd pair – you would imagine a scholar of the Bloomsbury Group to have a more refined pet – but the link is Sue's hulking and taciturn husband Wilf, a carpet layer, who came in a package with Horace. This explanation goes only so far, Sue and Wilf being just as odd a pair.

Horace is keen on ball games. When the four of us went for a walk on Hampstead Heath, we passed two small boys playing football. Horace muscled in, pressing his teeth into the ball and causing it to deflate. Both boys started to cry. Wilf went up to their father, another white-van man, to offer to pay for the ball, but the latter was unimpressed by the former's charade of remorse. 'I'll burst *your* fuckin balls, mate, if you don't keep your fuckin dog under control,' the father said. Wilf clenched his fists and a glint appeared in his eye. 'You keep yourself under fuckin control, mate,' he replied. Sue, foreseeing what the police call 'a situation', intervened with a five-pound note, some sweeties and a soothing word, and led Wilf and Horace away. She has the steely languor of an officer from *Zulu*.

Rottweilers have a reputation for ferocity, but Horace is simply full of beans. For a truly ferocious dog you should come to our village in Dorset and meet Bonkers, a Siberian husky who belongs to Old Luke, a ninety-four-year-old. The man is sofa-bound, and so the dog's only exercise is to prowl around the small garden of their bungalow. A public footpath runs past this garden, and when I was new to the village I strolled down it. Bonkers barked frenziedly at me and, as there was a high fence between us, I barked back. In a jiffy he was over the fence and had sunk his teeth into my thigh. My trousers notwithstanding, there was a semicircle of tooth marks in my skin for a fortnight. I thought of complaining to Old Luke, but he's gaga. Now, when passing the bungalow, I carry a rock. I gave up the footpath when I found that, if you get past Bonkers, there's a bull waiting in the next field.

A path with fewer deterrents leads through some meadows down to the river, a mile from the village. There I was dreamily gazing at a long-legged fly when I was disturbed by the rumble of a helicopter. I shook my fist at it, for the police helicopters that circle over our area in London are a blight, and we bought our cottage to escape such things. This helicopter hovered over the village, descended and disappeared behind some trees. Twenty minutes later, it rose again and flew off. When I returned from my walk, the high street was bubbling with gossip: a small girl had wandered up Old Luke's drive, Bonkers had ripped her face off, and the helicopter was an ambulance taking her to a specialist unit. That, we all assumed with relief, would be the end of Bonkers, but he is still at large; the only change is that now he wears a muzzle – on the odd occasions when Old L remembers to put it on him. As before, Bonkers sometimes escapes from the garden and wanders round the village. When this happens, the street is otherwise deserted. It's like the two tigers at Oxford Circus.

Old Luke is too doddery to think of entering Bonkers for any of the dog competitions that abound in Dorset during the summer; if there were a prize for the fiercest, Bonkers would win *cum laude*. The most serious competition is the one at Buckham Down Fair, which offers a number of categories, including Class B Bitch of the Year. I suggested to my wife Fluffy that she try for this; it didn't go down well. At the entrance to the fair we were queuing behind an elderly and genteel couple with their red setter, whom they said they were planning to enter for one of the prizes. The wait was long, the dog wanted a crap, he squatted down, and the woman nodded to her husband, who, plastic bag in hand, bent down behind the dog in readiness. A quart of diarrhoea was expelled under pressure, spraying the husband's shoes and narrowly missing mine. 'Oh dear,' the man mumbled, 'I don't think he's very well.' The couple exchanged pinched smiles. The aromatic puddle was not collectable in a plastic bag, and so they left it for us to stand beside. My mind went back to my cousin's whippet puppy Gertrude, who, when I was a child, burrowed into bed with me and exploded over my feet – *chienlit* in de Gaulle's sense.

Dog competitions are an attraction at our village fête. At a meeting of the organising committee, I proposed adding a cat show, in the hope that Maud would pick up some rosettes, but I was shouted down for various flimsy reasons. The fête lacks Buckham's *esprit de sérieux*: prizes are offered for, *inter alia*, Waggiest Tail, Loveliest Eyes and Oddest Couple – the last being won by a Bassett and a Pekingese. Stylish Owner went to an ungovernable teenager known as Shazza, who removed her bra before dragging her cur around the ring. Her stilletos sank in the grass. Best In Show was Maxine, the collie of Sam, a friend of mine who was visiting. Sam was unbearably smug for the rest of the day, and also failed to stop Maxine from chasing Maud in Maud's own house. Maxine seemed to think that Maud was a sheep in need of rounding up. The barking and hissing over, we confined them to separate rooms, but there were several near-misses when doors were opened. Feydeau could have made something of it. For most of the evening the two animals sat pressed, at red alert, against opposite sides of the sitting-room door, with only one inch between them. Dog-owning visitors blithely assume that Maud and I won't mind if the dog comes too. They are wrong, but we don't say anything.

As no prize is offered for Most Decrepit Dog, our elderly neighbours Henry and Eileen Tombs don't enter either of their dogs at the fête. Both animals are from a rescue centre, and one is blind, the other deaf: the Tombses are soft-hearted and rise to a challenge. The blind dog, Lizzy, was imprisoned for many years in a small cage, and got so used to it that now she is loth to move more than a few inches in any direction. Walks are out of the question. The deaf one, Charlie, likes to grind pebbles with his teeth, which have been reduced to smooth stumps. The four of them lived quietly and harmoniously till Eileen decided to add a stray kitten to the menagerie. She christened him Othello, for the obvious reason. Even for a kitten, Othello is hyperactive: he tears around the house, tears the furniture, and makes life misery for the dogs. When I dropped in, it was bedlam: Othello was on the rampage; Lizzy, unable to work out what was going on, was standing in the corner howling; and Charlie, who had been shut outside to avoid bloodshed, was barking speculatively through the cat flap.

At least the sensory handicaps are distributed between the dogs. My friend Andrew has a very old dog, Towser, a bloodhound, who is both blind and deaf – a terrible affliction, but less awful for a dog than for a human, as smell will take a dog a fair way: Towser stands up and wags his tail when you approach. Andrew owns another ancient dog, a retriever called Tray, who, although crippled with arthritis, could get about more quickly than Towser. Andrew therefore had to take them for separate walks. As Tray's arthritis worsened, Towser caught up, so there was a period when the three of them went out together; but, the decline continuing, Towser moved into the lead, and separate walks were resumed, but for the opposite reason. A graph could have shown the melancholy intersection of their curves of velocity.

Andrew, a true dog person, adores his two companions. When I was staying with them all in Paris – Andrew works there as a correspondent for a newspaper – I walked into the sitting room one morning and found him and Towser lying on the floor in an embrace. For a half-second I thought it was sexual congress. Before Paris, the three of them had lived in Delhi; when Andrew was transferred, he drove the dogs overland, in easy stages, to spare them the trauma of a flight. You might think a road trip of that length, with its changes of scene and climate, would be more upsetting, given their ages and disabilities. Recently a vet told Andrew that Towser's sight, but not his hearing, could be restored for £8,000. I suggested that, given the dog's great age, it was not worth it. Our friendship cooled from that moment.

One thinks more often of sighted dogs leading blind people. I knew a retired guide dog, a German Shepherd called Major: for some reason dogs of this breed often have army ranks for names. Major farted a lot, and had perhaps been trained to do so, in order for his blind owner, Karen, to locate him. German Shepherds are, I am told, rarely used as guide dogs these days, for their dodgy hips often shorten their career, but Major had been sacked for excessive initiative: when out with Karen, he would decide the itinerary. On the way to the office, Karen realised that they were in the wrong place. 'Where are we?' she called into the dark. 'The butcher's shop' was the reply. I have likewise seen a guide dog lead its owner a dance round King's Cross Station: they went up and down five platforms before reaching the exit. That was probably simple ignorance: having just got off a train from Aberdeen, how was the dog to know where to go?

An increasing variety of conditions have dogs to go with them. A neighbour working with people who are, like Towser, both blind and deaf tells me that they too have guide dogs. If the fire alarm goes, the dog lies across the owner's feet – not the best of signals, you might think, for with a dog across your feet it's hard to rush from the premises, especially if you are deaf and blind to start with. An agoraphobic friend was allotted an agoraphobia dog. It is obscure how such a dog differs from an ordinary one: you go out with the former, but then you do with the latter. Perhaps the point is that, whereas you accompany an ordinary dog, an agoraphobia dog accompanies you – but the distinction is a fine one, doubtfully discernible by the canine brain.

In the park I encountered a dog with a sign on its back saying 'Autism Dog': it loped up, dropped a ball in front of me and gazed into my eyes, presumably asking me to throw it. I wondered whether the dog itself was autistic and, if so, how you could tell. (Remember that telly programme about swans with brain damage?) My wife's take was that it was trained to look for autistic types and, when it found one, announced the discovery by dropping a ball in front of the person concerned. Fluffy likes to claim that I am autistic, and calls me Auty: it is her rejoinder to my righteous complaints about her untidiness – itself of such a degree as to indicate mental disorder. If I really were autistic, I would not want my dog to advertise the fact – or so I imagine; perhaps autistic people don't mind.

Down the Tube

The best birthday present my wife Fluffy ever gave me was to arrange a ride in a driver's cab on the Northern Line. The worst was a stuffed 'lion cub', which she had bought in Spitalfields market: it was obviously no such thing, but a guinea pig or rat that had been stretched and trimmed by an entrepreneurial taxidermist, and it was disintegrating – infested by weevils or similar. The second-worst present was a voucher for colonic irrigation. A voucher is unnecessary for the process, if a former student of mine is to be believed: he claimed to have irrigated his own colon by attaching one end of a hose to a bath tap, inserting the other in his bottom, turning the tap, and standing on his head to encourage the flow. Determined not to use Fluffy's present, I phoned Vera, my GP, and asked whether CI might be a bad idea, given that I had a heart murmur. It was a bad idea *sans phrase*, she replied, and I relayed her opinion to Fluffy. 'Without strawberries?' Fluffy queried. Never mind, she said: she could swap the voucher for one that would enable us to share a Mud Bath and Complete Body Cleanse – a contradictory combination, to my mind.

I had narrowly missed a shared mud bath some years previously in Budapest, where my friend Hamish took me for one in the basement of the Gellért Hotel. He had not, it is true, realised that the sessions were shared, or that, as a sign made clear, they were available only to Hungarian invalids accompanied by their doctors. We thought of passing ourselves off as such a pair, but I spoke no Hungarian, and Hamish's was limited to some irrelevant phrases from the *Time Out* guide to the city. Although the sign's wording was obscure in some respects – Did the invalid's doctor have the bath too? Would he want to share one with the invalid? – we were clearly excluded, so we settled instead for a massage and a dip in the thermal pool. There was only one changing cubicle free, which we agreed to share. Squeezed into a small space with a naked, obese and clumsy man, I was relieved that the experience was fleeting and that mud was off the menu.

The session with Fluffy, which took place in a 'spa' off Bond Street, was less traumatic than the one with Hamish would have been. A girl called Yvonne handed us our mud packs and, once we had put on robes, led us to a private steam-and-shower room which had murals of mermaids. Once we had mudded ourselves up like Black and White Minstrels, we contemplated congress on the floor, but the nonslip surface was too scratchy to lie on. 'You both look *lovely!*' Yvonne gushed, from script, when we emerged pink and perspiring.

Although I evaded colonic irrigation, my back end was penetrated in the course of a colonoscopy, which I was advised to have after a bout of piles. I suffer from these now and then, but they are usually relieved by Anusol, which, for an obvious reason, I prefer to buy at a self-service chemist. It was not on display in the small Boots near our country cottage, so in a whisper I asked the lady behind the counter whether she had anything for piles. 'Internal or external?' she thundered. I had never pondered the distinction. When I put my finger in my bottom, I could feel something squidgy, but it was not dangling out, so I ventured 'internal', which seemed less appalling.

Anusol failed to do the trick when, after a trip to Kenya, I found myself bleeding liberally during defecation. Vera prescribed suppositories, which I had never used. To insert one, she explained, you stand with one foot up on the side of the bath: that slightly opens your hole, into which you then push the thing. I was wondering what would keep it in after you had pushed, but when I tried I found that, once the suppository was nearly in, it was sucked the rest of the way by a mysterious force. Inside you it dissolved, which made farting hazardous: at a drinks party, while talking to a judge, I gently broke wind and filled my pants with an evil froth. Fortunately the party was at our house, so I broke the conversation off as politely as I could and rushed upstairs to change before the stuff seeped through to my trousers. During my suppository phase, I kept a spare pair of pants ready to hand at all times, and ran through my complete stock every couple of days.

The bleeding continued, so Vera referred me to Dr Watson, a colorectal specialist. You can't envy such people their job; perhaps the weakest medical students end up doing it – ditto feet and psychiatry. Watson seemed competent, however, and happy in his work. He announced that he was going to band my piles, i.e. put an elastic band round the swollen vein so as to choke off the blood supply and thereby cause the vein to wither. I heard myself ask Watson whether the procedure was elementary. Wearily, he invited me to pull down my pants and lie on the couch in a foetal position, facing the wall. Once curled up, I heard the rumbling of wheels – the banding machine, hitherto hidden behind a curtain, being trundled out. The process, which included suckings and poppings, was tolerable, but I felt queer afterwards in a way hard to describe: not a physical pain, more an existential ache. The treatment was a success and, when I went for a check-up, I told Watson that I and my friend David Capel, another of his patients, had spoken warmly of him. The name didn't ring a bell. 'Fair-haired man with big glasses,' I said. 'I'm not good with faces,' Watson replied.

He advised me to make an appointment for him to carry out a colonoscopy, to check that everything else was OK in what he called 'the nether world'. This involves inserting through the anus a small camera, which is pushed, on a flexible tube, along the

bowel to look for tumours and the like. In order for
the camera to see whether your bowel is sound, the
latter needs to be empty and sparkling clean, and so,
the day before, you fast and take strong laxatives. I
took the first dose after breakfast, and a couple of
hours later at the office I had a loose movement –
nothing to write home about, and in any event I was
going home at lunchtime, thinking it safer to work
there in case of little accidents such as those caused
by the suppositories. When I got back and Fluffy
asked for a progress report, I said I couldn't
understand why people made such a fuss. After
lunch I took the next dose, went up to my study, and
carried on drafting a legal opinion. An hour later, I
realised that I had soiled myself, and that watery
diarrhoea had soaked through my pants, not only
into my trousers but into the cushion of my chair.
Thereafter it was pandemonium, and I spent the rest
of the afternoon tearing between study and lavatory.
In the evening, feeling weak, I decided to watch a
DVD, and invited Fluffy to join me on the sofa. She
was understandably cautious, and agreed on
condition that I sat on a bin liner, but she became
tetchy because I kept pausing the film for more
emergency trips.

That night, in bed on more bin liners, I had
almost no sleep. What with that and the fasting, I
was lightheaded the following morning when I went
to the hospital for the probe. You are conscious
during the procedure, but they inject a relaxant into
your hand: I believe it is Rohypnol, the date-rape
drug. As soon as it went in, I felt a delicious

sensation – better than a large dry Martini – and I asked Watson where I could get more of the stuff. Behind his mask he laughed my question off, as Vera had once jovially dismissed my request for an easy, certain and painless means of suicide. Then it was the foetal position again, from which I could see the screen showing the view from the camera as it went along my insides. It was like that from the cab of the Northern Line train, only the sides of the tunnel were pink and squashy, and there were no stations. When the camera had to round a sharp bend, Watson's two assistants would unceremoniously yank my hips about. At the end of the journey – the colonic High Barnet – Watson said 'Lovely, a pristine bowel in perfect order.' I don't know what the protocol would have been if, in the course of the exploration, they – and I, watching the screen – had encountered a growth.

I was wheeled to Recovery, where I was given some excellent tomato sandwiches, better than they needed to be to satisfy a man who had fasted for twenty-four hours – but then it was a private hospital, as you could tell from the patients, most of whom were Arabs. I chose the sandwiches from a menu on which some items were marked 'healthy option': why would a hospital include unhealthy ones? As I was leaving, Watson gave me, for a souvenir, two photos of my bowel. One, showing its mouth, seemed to depict a toothless pink shark. I show it to visitors and ask them to guess what it is.

Upper Class

I profess indifference to badges of rank, but in truth I would be tickled to be Sir Oliver, or Lord Black. As things are, and are certain to remain, I must settle for being a doctor and a professor: they hardly count as titles, but they gave me pleasure when they came my way – the doctorate in particular, for I was young then and still capable of joy. In the months following the award of my PhD, I would announce myself whenever possible as Dr Black, causing confusion at medical appointments, and I would write 'Dr' on application forms for parking permits and other things to which my scholarly status was irrelevant. I kept this up until I overheard one of my friends from graduate school say to another that it was the sign of a wally to use academic titles outside the academy; he may have spitefully intended me to overhear, for his own thesis had been referred – i.e. he had been told to go away and rewrite it – and he therefore couldn't join my spree of self-inflation.

When I was made a professor a few years ago, the glow it induced was cooler, partly because of the points just rehearsed about joy and wallydom, partly because I was only a visiting professor and feared that 'visiting' might be *alienans* – that it might do to 'professor' what 'fool's' does to 'gold', 'toy' to 'mouse', and 'mock' to 'turtle soup' – and partly because by that time professorships had been dumbed down, 'professor' by then meaning roughly what 'senior lecturer' had once meant. So I stand to my professorial rank as Montaigne said he did to the Order of St Michael: instead of ascending to it, I waited for it to descend to me. But I make the most of the material I have, dropping the professorship into the conversation now and then (I leave out the 'visiting') and keeping my college security card in the front of my wallet, so that 'Professor Oliver' is on display ('Black' is obscured by the pocket).

The Oedipal basis, and consequent strength, of my desire for a proper title was recently brought home to me by a dream. An official tells me that in the next New Year's Honours I am to be made Dame Oliver Black. That's very nice, I say, but couldn't I be *Sir* Oliver Black? The official says he'll see what he can do. I reflect gleefully that, if I receive a knighthood, I'll be Professor Sir Oliver Black and shall thus have caught up with my father, who was Professor Sir Misha Black. The official comes back and says he's sorry, but it will have to be Dame Oliver.

The bit about my father was true: an eminent

designer, he was a professor at the Royal College of Art and was knighted for his *res gestae*. My mother and I accompanied him to the ceremony at Buckingham Palace, and for the occasion I wore a maroon denim suit with flared trousers (it was 1972 and I was fifteen). The trousers were not built to last: as I got into the limo, the crotch split from end to end, and I spent the morning with my thighs pressed together. The ceremony was pleasant, with a palm-court orchestra playing on a balcony, but the Queen was so far away that all we could see of her was a green blob, and, before she got round to knighting, we had to wait for hours while she dished out MBEs and other gewgaws; one of these was received by a miner, whose mates were sitting behind us and became rowdy. When we emerged from the Palace, the chauffeur couldn't start the car and had to ask a flunkey for a phone to call the garage. The mechanic he spoke to asked him where he was. 'In the forecourt of Buckingham Palace,' he replied. – 'Ha ha, we've heard that one before, mate.' We left him to it and caught the bus home. 'Drive us to Smallbone Mansions, Gloucester Road,' I called to the conductor, having read that a toff had once come out with something similar. My father apologised for me.

Excitement about the knighthood spread wide. It infected our cleaning lady, Mrs Round, who answered the phone in our flat when it rang the following day. 'Can I speak to Mr Black?' the caller asked. 'There's no one of that name here,' Mrs R replied, discounting me, and hung up. It also infected my father's office 'boy', an octogenarian called Ken. When, a few days after the trip to the Palace, Misha pointed out to him that the gents was running low in lavatory paper, Ken brought a roll of Izal Medicated to Misha's office on a stainless steel tray – the nearest he could manage to a silver salver. He bowed with one hand behind his back, like a footman, as he presented it. Less fazed was a Spanish waiter at Misha's club, for this man was under the impression that 'Misha' was itself a title (along the lines of Monsignor) which my father had long possessed. 'Good evening, Misha Black,' he would say in Quaker fashion.

The excitement trumped my adolescent *je m'en foutisme*. I tried to persuade my friends that by virtue of Misha's knighthood I had a courtesy title and that they should henceforth address me as Sir Oliver. They were not convinced, being less gullible than a girlfriend I had much later, who believed me when I said that I was a black belt in judo and that I could execute a triple somersault from a high diving board. She smelt a rat after I told her that I had been Head Boy at Eton – a school I never attended. 'Were you in Pop?' she replied, conversant as she was with Etonian arcana. 'No, but I was in Pip,' I hazarded. That blew it.

My mother, of course, really did gain a title via my father's. A precocious metaphysician, I assured her that she had undergone only a 'Cambridge change', but the claim was debatable and, even had it not passed her by, would have done nothing to mar either her passing and acute delight in the change –

which I caught her dancing a hornpipe to celebrate (she had been in the Wrens during the war) – or her lasting and subacute one in the resultant state. When Misha died a few years later, she altered our entry in the phone book to 'Black, Lady', which many people, failing to spot the comma, took to be the name of a pub. I'm told that the Duchess of Richmond has a similar problem. 'Do you do functions?' one caller asked me when I picked up the phone. 'Mathematical or bodily?' I replied, for I was a smart Alec and had tired of these intrusions. Other callers interpreted 'Black, Lady' differently and would just breathe heavily. My mother would have got more of the same, or worse, had I not persuaded her to reword the advertisement for language coaching that she was proposing to put in the local paper: 'Lady Black, French lessons'.

She was prickly about her ladyship, giving short shrift to her friend Peggy, who, when the knighthood was announced, said 'Of course, people scoff, don't they, but I'm so glad you're going to be a Lady.' Peggy then curtsied ironically. 'I haven't heard anyone scoff,' my mother replied tartly. She was also sharp with a neighbour, a taxi driver, who innocently asked her if she was Lady Jane Grey. My mother's first name was Joan and her surname was Black, so you can see how the confusion arose. In my experience such prickliness is characteristic of parvenu ladies. I once lodged with Annette Orr, relict of a man who had been ennobled for sucking up to royalty: when I wrote 'Lady Orr' on the rent cheque, she told me to change it to 'The Lady Orr', and became nasty when I suggested that she would be able to cash the cheque as it stood.[1]

It would be unfair to say that my mother had done nothing to earn her title, for she had run the household and endured neglect from Misha while he workaholically pursued the career that issued in his knighthood; but she had done nothing *directly* to earn it. Keen as I am to be Sir Oliver or grander, I have never been keen enough to put in the necessary direct grind. For a lawyer, which I was, there is a well-defined, if pot-holed and gate-ridden, path to a knighthood: you work your way to being a High Court judge and receive one *ex officio*. Had I been serious, I would have been a barrister rather than a solicitor, for the Bench is usually drawn from the Bar; but in any event, on the only occasion when I saw a High Court judge in action, I realised that a knighthood thus attained was not worth the candle. The old boy was sitting alone, trying a case about the defective construction of a car park in Thurrock. There being a lot of money at stake, the parties were represented by eminent QCs. Having looked forward to the glittering eloquence of Cicero and the laser-like analysis of Perry Mason, I was shocked by the barristers' fumbling grasp of their material and by their mumbling delivery of it. One of them had a speech impediment. These failings by themselves would have taxed the concentration of the judge, but in addition the facts, mainly concerning the

---

[1] I should have been warned off by her conduct when I first went to view the room: the previous lodger was still in residence, and The Lady shook her fist at him whenever he turned his back.

composition of some cement, were numbingly dreary. He could have nodded off if all he had needed to do at the end was say 'I find for the defendant,' but he had to write a judgment explaining his reasons, and that meant taking this ghastly stuff in. The silk with the impediment pronounced his j's as 'dr': 'That claim is undrustified,' he said, and other things similar. When he mentioned 'the drudge', he was spot on.

It's no wonder that judges like to let off steam once their robes are off. My wife Fluffy and I were invited to a judge's birthday party. When we realised that we were the only untitled couple at the table, we felt like Mr and Mrs Pooter at the Lord Mayor's reception, but we were put at our ease by the childish carrying-on of our *convives*, who had a long-running competition to insert obscure words into their judgments. '*I* used "hendiadys",' boasted one. '*I* got in "maieutic",' another countered. A third was hooted because his word was not obscure enough. (Mr Pooter: 'Carrie and I roared.') The word being 'homunculus', I wondered what the case had been about. The conversation then degenerated into a debate, increasingly ill-tempered, over the pronunciation of 'aposiopesis'.

In the old days, if you reached the top of the judicial tree, you joined the House of Lords. These days it's the Supreme Court, but you can still call yourself Lord X if you're one of the Justices and a man. Some lawyers are members of the House of Lords for other reasons; one such is Anthony Lester, styled Baron Lester of Herne Hill (my mother's neighbour would have styled him Baron Hernia of

Leicester Square), who kindly took Fluffy and me to the House to watch a debate. I was impressed by the courtesy of the proceedings, and by the fact that the noble debaters regulated their exchanges without umpiring from the Lord Speaker – on the other hand, emotions were unlikely to run high, given the subject matter (something to do with exemptions from EU regulations on the discharge of sewage) – but I was saddened to reflect that here they were at nine forty-five at night, beavering away, when they could have been at home in front of the telly. The poor things were for the most part well past their first bloom: true, the elderly are often wider awake at night than in the afternoon, but that was no reason to exploit these lovely old dears with a punishing regime of shift work. As with judging, the labour seemed to me too high a price for the title.

No, you don't want to earn a title: if possible, you should inherit it. That will not happen to me – absent an outlandish chain of disasters which, if long enough, would, I suppose, bring me to the throne. My friend Dan, who was brought up in an inter-war semi in Dollis Hill by parents who ran a café, claims to be 454th in line, but I have never grasped his reasons, and the claim is implausible, for he is Jewish. By scrimping, his father managed to send him to the John Lyon School, which is near the grander Harrow School; Dan and his friends used to cut through the grounds of Harrow, and once, when they were being boisterous, a Harrow boy shouted from the window 'Just because you're poor, there's no need to make that infernal din!'[2]

Although Dan has not inherited the throne, or anything else, he married into (and then divorced out of) the upper class. 'Upper class' is a term easier to apply than to define. To have a title is a sign, but not a sufficient condition, of being upper class: Misha was an Azeri immigrant raised in the East End. Nor is it a necessary condition. Dan's ex-wife Amelia,[3] undoubtedly upper-class (she described herself as such on a census form), is the granddaughter, on her mother's side, of an Earl, and her father was a cousin of the same Earl, but Amelia herself has no title.

To have a lot of money is likewise a sign but of course neither sufficient nor necessary. As to the insufficiency, pick a celebrity oik from *Mail Online*. As to the lack of necessity, take my friend the Hon Felicity Greaves, a scion of old nobility who draws the dole and lives in a one-bedroom flat in Ponders End. She was mortified when a visiting aunt, helping her to prepare supper in the kitchenette, asked 'Is this your *only* kitchen?' I once took Felicity and some others to stay in a sixteenth-century gatehouse let by the Landmark Trust. The rest of the party were

---

[2] My own schooling spanned the social spectrum. The nursery school, St Leonard's, was open to the local urchins, who taught me to shout 'Fuckin Boosticks' in public places. 'You'll have trouble with him, love,' an onlooker told my mother after one of these outbursts. My pre-prep school was Wetherby, where the pupils sported grey blazers with peach-coloured piping. Prince William – or was it the other one? – later went there.

[3] Odd that people should give the name to their daughters. 'Amelia', according to Chambers, means 'a congenital condition in which one or more limbs are completely absent'. Dan's Amelia, so far as I have been able to see, doesn't suffer from that condition.

delighted with it, but Felicity was sour because, she said, she should have inherited the big house at the end of the drive. This pile was open to the public; Felicity, who did not see herself as belonging to that category, took some cajoling to join a guided tour. On doing so, she was enraged to find the place occupied solely by her drunken cousin Willy (who briefly poked his unshaven face round the door and leered at us) and almost derelict. The great hall was lit by a solitary 100-watt bulb, making it hard to see the *pièce de résistance*, some splending carving by Gibbons. 'I can't believe monkeys done that,' one of the other members of the public exclaimed.

Perhaps a serviceable definition of 'upper-class' is 'closely enough related to someone with an inherited title that goes back at least several generations'; but the question needn't detain us, for on the whole you know the type when you see it. I had seldom seen it until Dan married Amelia, although I had caught some glimpses of it at Cambridge. There was the flat-capped beagling brigade at Magdalene, and my own college had a drinking society called the Elves, which had its share of the Hons. To my surprise I was invited to join this club and, seeing no strong reason to decline, went through the initiation ceremony, which involved the members' baring their buttocks while I drank a special cocktail – a pint of brown liquid comprising a double measure each of whisky, gin, rum and Pernod, topped up with Guinness and Worcester Sauce. This resulted in an almost instant loss of consciousness, followed shortly after, I am told, by projectile vomiting. When I awoke, in a strange bed, I directed my remaining heaves into the wastepaper basket that had been left within reach, but the basket was of open wickerwork, and so my thin and frothy chyme ran straight on to the rug. The basket was in any case a deckchair on the Titanic, for the more viscous product of previous heaves was still crawling down the wall.

While an undergraduate I was briefly the squeeze of a girl called Elsie, who was the daughter of a Scottish baronet, Sir Duncan Hamilton-Cairnes. Elsie and her sisters had been reared in the family castle, but, when the girls had all left home, Lady H-C – reputedly the most frightening woman in Fife – tired of running the place and paid the army to blow it up with mines. I asked Elsie whether they could not have donated it to the National Trust, or sold it for conversion into a hotel, but she replied that castles were ten-a-penny in Scotland. You can verify her reply, next time you are in the dentist's waiting room, by leafing through the property advertisements in *Country Life*: a Scottish castle, complete with grounds and shooting rights, can be picked up for the price of Felicity's flat in Ponders End. Since Felicity is so touchy about where she lives, I'm surprised that she has not made the swap.

To visit Sir Duncan and Lady Hamilton-Cairnes, as I once did with Elsie, was therefore a disconcerting experience: you drove through a magnificent gateway, its stone carved into fiery griffins, up a tree-lined drive half a mile long, and at the end, where the castle had been, was a small bungalow surrounded by rubble. We pressed the doorbell, which went ding-dong, and were greeted by Lady H-C, who showed us into what she disproportionately called the drawing room. She didn't immediately frighten me, but that may have been because it was hard to hear what she was saying, for Sir Duncan was practising the bagpipes in the guest bedroom. Presumably, when the castle had been standing, they had shut him in a tower for these sessions. A sporting man, he instructed all his daughters to 'make sure you marry someone who can shoot'. Elsie complied years later by marrying a US marine, who was cubic with muscle and seemingly slow-witted, but Elsie assured me that, if she disturbed him in his sleep, he would leap out of bed and adopt combat posture in two seconds. I lost touch with them when they moved to North Carolina to be near a marine base; my last letter from Elsie told me that they were living next door to a Pentecostalist preacher who had killed his wife with a bow and arrow. It was unclear why this man was at large: perhaps the proximity of the marines held him in check.

Elsie herself was accomplished in martial arts of a different sort, having studied some esoteric discipline during a period in Japan. Her master, she claimed, could set fire to a wad of cotton wool at a distance of several yards by flinging his arms towards it and yelling 'Zzzzaaaa!'; could cause assailants to fall over backwards by shrieking 'Aaaaaaaaiiiiiiii!' at them; and could turn glasses of water upside down without spilling any. This third claim was beyond belief – I felt sure that cling film was involved, as with that puerile prank some people play in the lavatory – but I gave Elsie the benefit of the doubt over the first two, and invited her to demonstrate the feats in question. She told me that they were far above her level, but she agreed to have a go, and so I dug some cotton-wool balls out of the bathroom cupboard (taking the opportunity, as I did so, to remind her of the chemist's riposte to the man who asks 'Do you have cotton-wool balls?'). The flailing of her arms was creditable, as was her 'Zzzzaaaa!', but the balls failed to burst into flames. Similarly, when I lunged, her 'Aaaaaaaaiiiiiiii!' failed to bring me to the ground. She saved face by tripping me up.

Once the courtship between Dan and Amelia was under way, she drove him to Norfolk to meet her mother, Lady Audrey Mallett. Audrey inhabited a Jacobean manor house, Farcombe Hall, which was approached through a series of arches along the drive. If these were designed to intimidate the visitor, the design worked on Dan, whose parents' house, in which he was still living, was reached by a twenty-foot path of crazy paving. Farcombe and its grounds were, as estate agents say, stunning, but had an ample share of blights. Norfolk is generally a dismal county, but it has its better and worse parts, and Farcombe was in one of the worst – only a river separating it from Gratting, a rapidly growing wasteland of Asdas, Lidls and Barratt Homes, with a Post Office that smelt of pee. Most of the residents were obese, the older ones parking their mobility scooters outside an inferno called the Dainty Café, which served fondant fancies and smelt more strongly of pee. Amelia called the town Grotting, and deplored the tattooed trespassers (she called them 'oaves' and said of them, as she did of many other things, that they were 'perfectly dreadful') who emerged from it to unleash their pit bulls and race their quad bikes on the levee on the Farcombe side of the river. (The levee was a necessity because Farcombe was below water level. Even with this protection, the place was engulfed every quarter-century or so when the river ran high.) With misplaced wistfulness, Amelia contrasted the town with Burnham Mark-Up, as she and her friends called Burnham Market – a Mecca for the affluent on the North Norfolk coast, where you can test your patience by queuing in specialist cheese shops while listening under duress to the other queuers shouting down their mobiles to their nannies; this place is also known as Hampstead-on-Sea.[4] On Tuesdays the snarls of the quad bikes on the Farcombe levee would be drowned for some hours by the shrieks of RAF fighters from the nearby base, and at night the skies continued to echo with the rumble of the local flour mill, the roar of the main road and the rattling of goods trains. Sounds are always more noticeable at night, but in the Fens they are made still more intrusive by the absence of hills between you and their sources. The same goes for light, Gratting casting up a bilious orange glow worthy of Vegas.

These inconveniences had not yet impinged on Dan when he was introduced to Audrey, so his praise

---

[4] Burnham Market – or was it Burnham-on-Crouch? – used to have a restaurant called The Burnham Grill. It was empty when I looked through the window.

of Farcombe was neither qualified nor feigned. 'We open the house and grounds to the public every month,' Audrey offhandedly replied. 'Do you open *yours* to the public?' Dan's mental cinema showed coachloads of respectful visitors tramping up the crazy paving, through the hall and kitchen, out of the back door and into the overgrown garden, where they formed a logjam and photographed a gnome. After Dan and Amelia were married, they spent a lot of time at Farcombe, and the suburban bloke eased into the role of squire, relishing his unofficial position as replacement for Amelia's late father. He would rise early to shoot rabbits, usually managing only to maim them and leaving them to drag themselves back to their holes, where they could die slowly. He got on well with Audrey, who put up with, and even put up, his friends, and I therefore became a frequent guest.

My first encounter with Audrey was no more comfortable than Dan's had been. The bedroom allotted to me was next to hers and, when Amelia showed me up, Audrey was on the landing in dressing gown and curlers. Not being ready to receive, she looked straight through me while holding a long conversation with Amelia about the arrangements for what they both called 'luncheon'. Hovering three feet away, I grinned weakly. Ten minutes later, and still before we had greeted each other, Audrey cut me again, when I walked into the lavatory and found her at stool. There being a working lock on the door, I speculated that it was bad form to use it and that one was meant to knock before entering. She gazed dreamily at nothing while I burbled 'Oops, sorry, oh dear,' and so on. When at last she condescended to speak to me – once we were downstairs and equipped with sherry – it was to ask whether I was one of the Somerset Blacks or a Staffordshire Black. 'Neither, I'm afraid,' I replied. 'A Cumberland Black?' she ventured, with a tincture of disdain. Deciding not to counter with the questions whether Cumberland still existed, and whether a Cumberland Black was a breed of pig (perhaps the one from which the sausages came), I settled for an apologetic shake of the head, whereupon she turned to another guest. Despite this cold start, we became friendly over my subsequent visits, although Audrey was always worried that I would stay too long. She may have thought I was a vagrant. 'Good Lord, are you moving in?' she cried with hollow jollity, seeing the king-size plastic Delsey suitcase that I once brought after my overnight bag had fallen to pieces. And, as soon as Sunday lunch was over, she would spontaneously cry 'You aren't going already?' with equally hollow dismay.

On the other hand, there was some evidence that she found my presence soothing, for I was always given that bedroom next to hers. The room, like most things in life, had its pros and its cons. The chief cons were (1) that the occupant was under Audrey's eye, a point to which I shall return, (2) that one of Farcombe's scruffy peacocks had just enough wing power to scrabble on to the window ledge, whence it would eye me balefully and emit a piercing wail like that of an infant being tortured (this peabrained bird, or one of its colleagues, once attacked my peacock-blue Ford Fiesta, which it

to me, lest she thought I was getting fresh) and with one ankle jauntily propped on the opposite knee. As always, tea was hard-core, with egg-and-cress sandwiches, crumpets, scones, and fondant fancies disturbingly similar to those in the Dainty Café. There were also some small jellies in crinkly paper cups, the sort you find at a sixth-birthday party. (Nursery food was frequent at Farcombe, despite the absence of children.) I seized the opportunity, for which I had waited years, to say 'May I press you to a jelly?' but failed to raise a titter.

Audrey took a dim view of it if you didn't stuff a lot down – a trial for me, given the state of my guts: I felt like a contestant at one of those competitions to swallow thirty pork pies in one minute. As she expected you to keep eating throughout the day, she blurred the boundaries between meals. Breakfast (Full English, including black pudding) segued into elevenses (coffee, biscuits and Dundee cake), which morphed into pre-lunch sherry and Pringles; lunch was hot, and included pudding and cheese; and no sooner had you woken from your post-lunch zizz than the gong, seldom silent, summoned you to tea of the kind just described. A short pause enabled you to take some bicarbonate of soda and dress for dinner, and then you were off again with three or four courses, followed by port and/or brandy. In case you felt peckish during the night, there was a box of shortbread biscuits under the bed. Perhaps in the old days people burnt it all off by hunting, but Audrey and Amelia, being sedentary, converted it into chins, thighs, buttocks and spare tyres. Dan was expanding, but was not yet in Amelia's league, let alone Audrey's. The only exercise Audrey took was occasionally to sit and bounce up and down for a few seconds on an antique device called the liver-jerker – a large cushion-cum-mattress with springs inside and mahogany handles to hold on to.

On my first visit I understood 'dress for dinner' to mean 'brush your hair and put on a different jersey'. That landed me in a Bateman cartoon when I went downstairs to find Dan and the other male guests in dinner jackets. I was consoled to reflect that my own DJ, had I brought it, would have shamed me almost as much as its absence was doing: bought from Marks and Spencer twenty years previously for an Elves jamboree, it had a vomit stain on the lapel, and the trousers – hurriedly turned up by my mother with a crude zigzagging stitch – reached no lower than my ankles. For my next visit to Farcombe I bought a more respectable outfit from Hackett, but I was still let down by my shirt and bow tie. The shirt, decades old, had belonged to Misha: it had been handmade for him by Sulka, but I am much longer and thinner than he was, and so the material billowed, the shoulders draped over my upper arms, the cuffs stopped two inches short of my wrists, and there was room for another neck in the collar. The superfine cotton had become diaphanously thin with age, revealing my nipples and threatening to rip when I reached for the gravy. The bow tie, also Misha's, was better preserved and fitted the collar, if not my neck, but I made a horlicks of tying it, and it obstinately settled at forty-five degrees between horizontal and vertical. When tucking the inner loop under my collar failed to solve the problem, I thought of Blu Tack, but none was handy. The root of the trouble was that I had been taught to tie these things by Misha, who was left-handed and had invented his own knot. I should have plumped for a clip-on one and resigned myself to looking like Ray McVay.

Meals in the dining room were marred by Bruno, an aged and overweight Labrador, who would settle under the table, whence his stink would mask every savour. Now and then he would overlay the general dogginess with a fart, sometimes audible, and your neighbour would think it was you, as in 'I sat by the Duchess at tea'. When overcome by desire for affection (which he seldom received) or for a titbit (which he often received), he would bury his muzzle in your privates and shake his head vigorously, making a bubbling sound and leaving your trousers slimy and rank. Amelia encouraged him by bending under the table and making him perform his party piece: 'Bruno, wag your tail,' she would say, and he would do so in response, of course, to the 'Bruno' and not to the 'wag your tail'. At one lunch I overheard a conversation between Audrey and Professor Wilbye, a Renaissance historian whom Dan had invited down: Wilbye was holding forth about the cosmology of Giordano Bruno, and Audrey, whose mind was far away, interjected 'Ah yes, poor Bruno, he's a smelly old thing, but we love him dearly.' She was prone to such misunderstandings: on another occasion Dan produced an aesthetician, whom Audrey asked for advice on the side effects of anaesthetics.

Bruno (the dog) used to leave man-sized turds in unexpected places throughout the house, a habit for which possible and connected explanations were (a) that he was senile, (b) that he was rarely taken for a walk, and (c) that unhappiness had caused him to exhibit challenging behaviour. With (b) in mind, I once took him on a ramble around the grounds, but I regretted my kindness, for he wandered into the path of an oncoming tractor which narrowly missed him. 'Keep your bloody dog under control!' the driver shouted, but control was impossible, for Bruno didn't have a lead or even a collar. It would have been pedantic to shout back that he was not my dog. Sometimes Bruno would escape from the house by himself: he would waddle off into the distance, and Audrey would receive a phone call hours later from whichever public-spirited person in the next village, or the next but one, had 'rescued' him. Some villagers were worse-disposed, one of them taking a pop at him with an air rifle, and thus removing part of his ear, for rummaging through a dustbin. On one desperate occasion in midwinter, Bruno swam the river and made it into Gratting, where he found his way to the Dainty Café. Perhaps he felt an affinity with its doddering patrons, or thought that, what with the reek of pee, no one would mind his own odours, now enriched with river mud.

Finally, when Audrey found a six-inch Bruno Special on her pillow – in the place where, in a fancy hotel, a chocolate mint would have lain – she saw red and decided to get rid of him. A retired schoolteacher and his wife agreed to take Bruno in,

Audrey having omitted to mention the incontinence
– a harsh application of *caveat adoptor*. Thereafter she
took pains to avoid the couple, but, when she bumped
into them at church, they were full of Bruno's praises
and said nothing about turds. 'He seemed depressed
at first,' the wife said, 'but now he's such a happy old
boy, and he loves a good long walk.' Her words
favoured explanations (b) and (c) over (a).

I enjoyed my Brunoless rambles, and was happy
wandering aimlessly, but Dan, keen to entertain and
impress, laid on clay-pigeon shooting, boating on the
lake, and other jollies. On the occasion of the clay
pigeons he offended me by standing behind me with
his arms out when I fired the shotgun. 'They have
quite a kick, these things,' he explained, 'and the blast
might knock you over backwards.' I'm slender, it's
true, but not a stick insect. After that I was grudging
in my agreement to provide a reference for him to
renew his gun licence. A few weeks later a
policewoman rang me and asked whether I thought
Dan a fit person to own a shotgun. She sounded
dissatisfied with my 'I suppose he's no less fit than
many who do', and went on to ask whether I was
aware of any history of mental illness in his family. It
was tempting to reply that his father was the Mad
Axeman of Dollis Hill, now in Broadmoor, but I
weakly gave Dan a clean bill, and so, with licence
renewed, he carried on idly amusing himself by
blasting the rear quarters off harmless creatures.

The outing on the lake, a case of two men in a
boat, was no more gratifying. Dan assumed, without
asking, that I would row, and I was content to do so,

having been in the Fourth Eight at school (I gave up after a report that read 'Is quite keen, but size and strength are limiting factors'); but there was no opportunity to display my prowess, for the lake was wholly covered in a luminous weed – bright and plentiful enough to be woven into hi-vis coats for all lollipop ladies – which clung to the oars. At best it was like rowing through green Bovril, and at worst progress was impossible, the boat merely rocking back and forth around a fixed point as I pulled and pushed. When, as exhausted as I had been after the Schools' Head of the River, I got us back into the little boathouse, Dan tipped the boat sideways while clambering out; he managed to hop unwetted on to the platform, but I ended standing in water up to my thighs. I squelched back to the house, the lurid weed on my trousers making me look like a character from a mystery play and smell worse than Bruno.

The only organised outdoor entertainment that I enjoyed at Farcombe was the annual play, which Dan would write for the nonce and which family and house guests would perform on a raised lawn. Five feet below was another lawn, and the two together served well as stage and auditorium. The groundlings were miscellaneous residents of the next village (no one from Gratting was admitted). One of these filmed our production of *Lady Audrey's Secret* – Dan was sailing close to the wind – and afterwards gave us a tape (it was those days) of the result. The picture was OK, but the camera's microphone had picked up the comments of the audience rather than the speeches of the actors. 'What a tosser,' a rustic voice said as I made my flamboyant entrance. Dan tried to reassure me that the man had been talking about Atossa, the mother of Xerxes, but it seemed unlikely.

It was on one of these dramatic occasions that I first met Fluffy, who at that time was a colleague of Dan's and whom he had enlisted to be stage manager. We were immediately attracted to each other, and she made it clear that she would welcome a visit from me that night. As we were at opposite ends of the house, it was a trek, and I was worried that, when I sneaked back the following morning to dress, I would bump into Audrey. To put her off the scent, on my return journey I stopped off at the lavatory with the detachable door, but when I emerged Audrey was scowling at me from the doorway of her bedroom. I strove to believe that the scowl was due to the small patch of pee on the front of my nightshirt, but it was pretty clear that she knew what was, so to say, up: quite probably she had put her head round my door, which I had negligently left open, and seen that the bed was untouched.

I was not going to let a censorious old cow block the road to rapture, so the following night, once all was quiet (save for the snoring of Bruno in the hall), I tossed my bedclothes about and then set off again in my nightie for Fluffy's chamber. As I turned into her corridor, a bell started clanging by my ear and a siren wailed outside. I hurried back towards my bedroom, passing other clanging bells, and encountering bleary and grumpy guests who were emerging from their rooms. On reaching my landing, I again found Audrey framed by her doorway and wearing the scowl with which she had greeted me in the morning. 'Have you been wandering around the house?' she asked me, in a voice she might have used to scold Bruno after one of his little accidents. I resorted to the now-standard weak grin. 'Christ Almighty,' she went on, 'the police will be here any minute.' Her statement was true in part: two squad cars did roll up on the gravel outside, but not until an hour later, by which time both the house and Audrey's manner were freezing. Politeness, and a sense of partial responsibility, moved me to sit up with her and Amelia (Dan went straight back to bed, and was soon snoring in counterpoint with Bruno), but sympathy for Audrey was not a motive, for it was obvious that she had set the alarm in order to teach me a lesson and had thus brought all this on herself.

The grandeur of life at Farcombe was smoke and mirrors, for Audrey was destitute and Amelia, her only child, was modestly paid for the gentle dabbling she performed in an auctioneer's African Art department. (A bar to her being promoted there was the accident she had caused when delivering a bunch of spears. She had tied them insecurely to the roof rack of her car and, when she stopped abruptly at traffic lights, they shot forward, penetrating the soft top, and grazing two occupants, of the car in front.) As no money flowed in from the wealthier reaches of the family, an adequate staff was out of the question: the only denizens of Downstairs were a live-in couple (more strictly, live-out, as they were housed in a primitive cottage – again more strictly, a sty – in the grounds) who did all the cleaning, shopping, cooking and serving, as well as keeping an eye on Audrey when Amelia was in London. 'A couple' here refers not to a single pair of old retainers, but to whichever couple currently occupied the post: their tenure was usually brief because, first, the conditions were bleak; second, people willing to do that sort of work tended to be strange and, when their strangeness became oppressive, Audrey would sack them – causing misery for Amelia, who would then have to ransack *The Lady* for replacements.

When I started visiting Farcombe, the incumbents were an ex-army cook and his wife. The cook, Gavin, produced food in the vast quantity required, enough for a regiment on active service, but the quality too was suited to the battlefield, and Audrey complained that some of the dishes he prepared were vulgar. Puzzlingly, she objected on that ground to trifle, but not to the jellies mentioned earlier. When I probed the distinction, she explained that the 'prublim' was not the trifle as such, but the fact that it contained jelly. This was *obscurum per obscurius*. Such niceties didn't endear her to Gavin, who was anyway so surly that visitors, and even Audrey and Amelia, were too frightened to enter the kitchen to fetch the bottled water that, as I had learnt the hard way, one was advised to drink. He would brood at the table, with a rolling pin and a two-litre bottle of extra-strong perry within reach. When once, and only once, I tried a pleasantry, he growled 'No one talks to me like that,' and his hand twitched in the direction of the rolling pin. His wife Linda, whom Audrey and Amelia called Hitler, was bossy rather than threatening. At one lunch she was moving round the table, holding a plate from which the diners could help themselves to liver and bacon, and whispering to each diner in turn 'Two portions for the gentlemen, one for the ladies.' The liver was rigid and the bacon flabby, so I took just one portion. '*Two* portions for the gentlemen, *one* for the ladies,' Linda hissed with greater emphasis, and I feebly complied. She and Gavin were given their cards after the latter was found shouting to himself in the woods at night.

Opening Farcombe to the public raised little more than pin money. To prevent the beetles from devouring the roof, the rising damp from reducing the skirtings to mush, the dry rot from transubstantiating the panelling into Ryvita, and the utilities from disconnecting all supplies, Audrey and Amelia were fain to let the place out for 'events', which usually meant weddings. I caught the end of one of these: a marquee had been erected, and in it a crowd of Hooray Henries and Sloanes were braying at each other while rain drummed on the roof. No one querying my presence, it occurred to me that, if you were down on your luck, you could fill yourself with goodies every Saturday in summer by tootling around the countryside and crashing whichever wedding reception you lit upon. From my wedding with Fluffy I know that bride and groom have no idea who many of the revellers are. 'Hallo,' a woman said to me on that occasion: 'remember me? I'm Veronica – Vanessa's sister.' I was sure we had never met before, and Vanessa didn't ring any bells.

Or take my experience at the Reform Club, where my friend Simon was having a party to launch his *Socage and Frankalmoin in Late Mediaeval Binstead* (University of Wales Press, £80). When I arrived, I asked the porter which room the party was in, and he directed me upstairs. The splendid saloon into which I strolled was full of the chic and affluent enjoying themselves: the champagne abounding, they were well-oiled, and conversation had reached shouting level. After drinking a few glasses, eating many scrummy canapés and nattering to various affable people, I asked one of these where Simon was. 'He's over there,' she replied, gesturing vaguely, and then asked 'Are you on the bride's side or the groom's?' The penny dropped. In any large English gathering there is likely to be someone called Simon, as I once confirmed by calling to my one when I saw him at the theatre: at least thirty men turned round. I was tempted to bluff on at the reception for the rest of the evening, for I was having such fun, but loyalty propelled me back downstairs to the porter, who apologetically redirected me to The Cold Room – a fluorescently lit hangar, which was empty, save for one corner in which a handful of miserably dressed academics (fuzzies, my wife calls them) murmured to each other over warm white wine and Hula Hoops. Everyone there seemed to be depressed. I could now see the right Simon, who introduced me to, and then scuttled away to leave me alone with, a blind historian of something called venville. I could get little more than a grunt out of this man, who was perhaps embittered by his handicap, and I was put off my Hulas by the rolling of his eyes; but I felt I couldn't abandon him, and he couldn't catch the eye of anyone else, so we were stuck with each other. Watching him knock back the disgusting plonk, I feared that he would soon ask me to lead him to the lavatory, and that I would mess it up, somehow causing him to step into the gutter of one of the Reform's majestic urinals.

I was more aware of the corner-cutting and penny-pinching at Farcombe after I was taken to visit 'the neighbours'. These I assumed to be some people in the next village, but it turned out that in Audrey's mouth the phrase meant the occupants of the nearest stately home, fifteen miles away. This was Wixoe Hall, and its chief occupant was Lord Arthur Gridley, who was known, for an obvious reason, as Fatty. Here was the real thing – a butler, footmen, and a nanny who whisked children away as soon as the little angels had been kissed and patted by the visitors. The occasion was a buffet lunch: I stood alone and ignored, clutching a plate of cold salmon and wondering whether Fatty and his guests took me to be a chauffeur who had been mistakenly admitted to the party. (At Amelia's request I had driven us over from Farcombe, and Fatty had seen me emerge from the driver's door.) Around me men in tweed jackets and brightly coloured cords bawled and were bawled at by women in frocks. Fatty was at my elbow, cheerily pouring inanities into the ear of an ancient lady whose lipstick was smeared around, rather than on, her lips, à la Coco the Clown. Some of it had strayed on to her false teeth – the expensive kind that are slightly uneven for the sake of verisimilitude; but hers were still too good to be true, behind lips so shrivelled. 'Y'know, I've got an *awfully* sorft spot for Venice,' Fatty was saying. In return the old thing gawped at him: her whistly hearing aid was giving her gyp, and she may have been gaga. Fatty, straining to fan a conversation into flame, turned to me and said 'Do *you* have an awfully sorft spot for Venice?' My brain emptied. There must have been a charming or witty reply, but I was dumbstruck, and so I pasted on the weak grin that I used for awkward moments with Audrey. Fatty applied something similar and, recognising that we were at a standstill, edged his way to another victim. As my brain juddered back into action, I pondered the shades of difference between his vowels and Audrey's, and wondered whether he had acquired his squeaky 'Y'know' at Eton. It seemed unlikely, for Fatty was surely too dim to have passed the entrance exam, but family may have done the trick. Other Etonians of my acquaintance like to start their sentences with a high-pitched and meaningless noise: one, a Conservative grandee, begins with 'Pip!' – or used to, before he was groomed for sound bites. I suppose it's a way of attracting attention.

My musing was interrupted by the sight of Amelia approaching with another ancient person – a powerfully built and patchily shaven man whom she introduced as Bunty, and who turned out to be the Earl of somewhere. I wondered whether all aristocrats had infantile nicknames. Amelia told me later that Bunty had been only fifth in line for the earldom, but that hereditary cretinism had prevented the intervening relations from inheriting. I was sceptical, for I had not heard that brains were necessary for a title, and a quick glance around the room supplied evidence to the contrary. Bunty himself seemed to have few marbles. When Amelia gushed 'Bunty darling, this is Oliver, who's staying with us at Farcombe,' he stared at me and bleated, a wild rictus revealing sparse and tawny fangs. No conversation ensuing, Amelia ushered him away, and I was left alone till it was time to leave. '*So* sorry we didn't have a proper chance to chat,' Fatty unconvincingly said to me on the doorstep. 'We *must* catch up next time.'

This was a case of 'If necessarily P, then not P' – a principle neglected by modal logicians: there was a next time, to my surprise and alarm, but on that occasion Fatty and I failed to do anything that would count as catching up. The format was different – a sit-down dinner – but the guests were a subset of those at the lunch, so I grimly looked forward to being blanked while conversation ranged over country sports and other alien topics. To fortify myself, I accepted every refill during the pre-dinner drinks; the footman being attentive, my glass, like the Queen's, was never empty, and after twenty minutes I was alternately swaying like a poplar in a breeze and leaning against the wall.

At table I was startled and, at first, pleased to find myself next to Cecilia Goslett, an intellectual historian whose presence was explained by her being, incongruously, married to a minor Royal. A beautiful woman, she smiled winningly at me as she crumbled her roll. Lured, I ventured a pretentious remark about dialectic, which, in my cups, I pronounced 'dialectric'. Her smile hardened. 'Are you talking about Platonic dialectic, Hegelian dialectic or Marxist dialectic,' she asked sternly, 'or do you mean dialectic in one of its Indian forms?' I tried to change into seminar gear, but was too far gone to find the mental clutch, so I lamely replied 'I suppose I mean what's common to all of them.' 'They have nothing interesting in common,' she retorted, and turned to the man on her other side, whom she proceeded to savage in the same way. I couldn't hear what he said to her, but I did catch her reply: 'What you've just said is stupid.' I wondered whether she took the same no-nonsense approach at the Palace and, if so, how it went down: Philip might give her marks for spunk, but the Queen would not be amused. It was a relief when the ladies retired and I was left next to a buffer coincidentally called Mr Black (perhaps *he* was a Cumberland Black). 'Fine weather we've been having,' he gurgled. Under normal conditions I would have groaned, but after the pasting I had received from Cecilia I was ready to fall on Mr Black's neck. He was drinking claret, and I wanted port, but I had to follow his lead as the bottles were passed round, for I wasn't sure which of the many glasses in front of me was the right one for port. Earlier in the meal I had been daunted by the profusion of outsized cutlery.

When Dan and Amelia separated, my door to the upper class shut, for Amelia wanted nothing more to do with her ex's cronies. I had enjoyed my visit, but was happy not to prolong it – just as, although you might relish a holiday in Goa, you wouldn't want to live in a straw hut by the sea all the year round. I still wish I were a middle-class Lord Black, but I'll have to go on wishing.

Two Wheels Better

When I was very small, my mother Joan used to take me and my tricycle to St James's Park, where I would tear along the lakeside path, my rear wheels millimetres from the bunions of the old ladies on the benches. They would whip their feet in as I passed. My memory of those days is generally dim, but I vividly recall the one on which Joan delegated her role to my half-brother Jake, who lost me near the pelicans. Screeching to a halt on the pavement opposite Horse Guards Parade, I found myself alone. I have not been more terrified.[1]

My transition from trike to bike was painful for

---

[1] Jake became an anthropologist and went to study nomads in Iran. Before setting off, he impressed me by announcing that, after driving into the wilds as far as he could, he would exchange his Volkswagen for a mule. Once the mule got him there, he lived with the nomads long enough to introduce a new word into their language. As he sat writing his notes, the children would irritate him by playing around his tent, and he would shout 'Fuck off!' Later he noticed that the people were using 'fukofi' to mean naughty.

Joan, who would hold me steady at the back while I tried to balance. Stabilising wheels had failed to do the trick. The bike being small, she had to bend low, and as I was a slow learner these backbreaking excursions were repeated over months. To speed things up, she would tell me what a thrilling moment it would be when I found I could stay upright on my own. I can remember the moment, but not the thrill, if there was one.

As a young man I cycled in London, but two incidents made me nervous of the traffic. On one of my rides I passed a street that had been cordoned off: on the tarmac was a twisted bicycle, a shoe and a small mound of red goo. Then Mandy, a friend from university who went barefoot, had one of his (sic) feet squashed by a lorry as he waited with his bike at a traffic light; scorning crutches, he hopped around in plaster for weeks after.[2] London now has dedicated cycle lanes, but other bikes are as great a menace as lorries. When, a couple of years ago, I rode down a lane near Mount Pleasant (ludicrously named), I was elbowed aside by overtakers, and had to swerve to avoid an oncoming cyclist whose speed combined with mine was over fifty miles an hour.

I was trying out a Brompton, which my wife Fluffy had ordered me to buy even though neither of us needed a bike. As it was secondhand, there were no instructions on folding and unfolding it. The steps were simple, but hard to work out for yourself, and the effort caused me to have tantrums. Finding

---

[2] In those days he was writing a thesis on nihilism. Years later when I encountered him he was a pensions adviser.

me hammering the pavement in rage, Fluffy led me to YouTube, where a nonchalant youth folded and unfolded his Brompton in a few seconds and then pedalled off with a wave. After following his motions a few times I got the hang of it, but I used the bike so rarely that I forgot the trick between outings. I have similar trouble with our central heating when autumn arrives.

Before the Brompton, Fluffy had urged me to buy an old tandem that was on sale in Spitalfields market. The likelihood that both of us would ever want to cycle at the same time, let alone to the same destination, was tiny, but, when the vendor – a depressed man called Hector who ran a leather-goods shop – offered us a test ride, I agreed to have a go, partly from curiosity and partly because, in the Black family, tandems have a romantic association, my father's brother Sam having courted Auntie Muriel on one in the 1930s.[3] My father, who stuck to walking, was at the time a pillar of the North London Jewish Ramblers – a small band, I imagine.

Hector's tandem, a tourer, was enormous. It may have belonged to the wearer of the uncannily long prosthetic leg that I had been unable to stop Fluffy from buying in the market the previous week. I have long legs, but was barely able to touch the ground from the saddle, and Fluffy could only wave her feet in the air. For that reason she agreed to sit at the back, but she was grumpy about it, because she is a bossy person and the backseater had no

---

[3] It was said that Muriel wore her slip under her bra on the wedding day, to bulk out her bosom.

control over the machine, their role being merely to provide power. I sensed, when we set off, that Fluffy was filling the role halfheartedly, but we were too wobbly for me to turn round and check whether she was applying herself: I needed to concentrate on the road ahead, for our ride, through the heart of the City, coincided with the evening rush hour.

Even with her limp contribution, it was clear that a tandem has much more oomph than a one-man bike. Had we lived in the Fens, we might have had fun from this one. As it promised only to clutter our hall, I declined the purchase. There was an outcry from Fluffy about my being unable to spot a bargain, to seize an opportunity, or to enjoy life, but she had forgotten the thing twenty-four hours later. She was now pestering me to open a tea shop and to invest in gold.

Joan's Fleet

I am old enough to remember Messerschmitts – not the wartime fighter planes, I'm pleased to say, but the bubble cars, made by the same company, which looked like cockpits cut out of the planes and stuck on to three small wheels. Every evening a man would park one of these in our street and sleep in it overnight. In the morning he would brush his hair and teeth in the rear-view mirror and drive off. As I was very young, I found it unremarkable.

In those days there were trolley buses in London. My friend Dan, who was also around at the time, insists that there weren't, but either he is forgetful or he was kept indoors, for I clearly remember taking them to visit Moomps and Poops, my father's parents, in Finsbury Park. Why, if I had never been on a trolley bus, would I have such a bright mental picture of its extra wheels, and of the conductor flailing around with a pole as he tried to re-attach an errant trolley to the overhead wires? I can also remember those diesel buses that had a vertical radiator and a little box right at the top, showing just the number. 'Face the future with PEARL assurance' was an advertisement commonly on the sides. If you see a photo from that period, it seems a remote age, but I was there, toddling around.

It was on one of the latter buses that my mother Joan used to take me to nursery school. One day when we were in my favourite seat, behind the driver's cab, the driver reached backwards out of his window, into the small opening at the top of mine, and handed me a boiled sweet. I was so impressed that, for months after, I would sit on the end of the small bed in our guest room, pretending to be the bus driver. 'I'm the driver, and you're Alwa [Oliver],' I would declare to Joan, who sat behind me and received an imaginary sweet. It's one of my happiest memories. Tears fill my eyes as I type. The amusements of adulthood are straw in comparison.

As we lived in central London, public transport met our needs, but when I was seven my parents decided that we should have a car. Joan would have to drive, for my father Misha, an industrial designer, was unable to – which was just as well, given his tendency to fall asleep; he did so on a bicycle, waking up as he hit the ground, and he also once nodded off giving a lecture. He had no idea of a car's controls. When, soon after we had bought the car, Joan got out to ask for directions, she forgot to put the handbrake on. The car started to roll backwards. 'The brake, the brake!' she shouted to Misha, whose head wobbled in panic as he gawped at the dashboard.

From the back seat I leant forward and pulled the handbrake. It is worrying to think that my father designed planes and locomotives. His understanding of the engine was just as cloudy. When we broke down and Joan went to phone the AA, Misha opened the bonnet and peered in, a lighted Gitane *Maïs* dangling from his lips, as it always did. (He was a constant fire-hazard; the Gitane would dangle there while he helped me with my chemistry set, smouldering ash dropping on to strips of magnesium ribbon.) It was all role-play, for he could not tell the carburettor from the dipstick. He might as well have been staring at a human brain.

I can't take the high ground here, for I am almost as ignorant of the internal combustion engine. At public school I attended a few lessons on the topic, but they were purely theoretical, given by a retired colonel known as Lordy, because he tended to cry 'Lordy!' in moments of stress. Such moments were frequent, Lordy being a soft target for practical jokes, the cruellest of which took place in one of his practical classes in metalwork. A thug called Charnage – who attached a firework to the leg of the headmaster's Jack Russell, inserted a cigarette into the anus of Matron's cat, and finally, before being expelled, nicked (or, as he put it, 'wogged') lead from the chapel roof and sold it in the local market (I wonder what became of him?) – heated a bar of iron to just under red-hot and then cozened Lordy into picking it up. 'Daaaaaaaaaaagh, Lordy!' bellowed Lordy, into the gale of merriment from the class. All I can remember from the lessons on car engines is a trick for telling whether your spark plug is working. Take the cap off and touch the top: if it's working it will give you an electric shock. 'May bump you orf if you have a dicky heart,' Lordy said, 'but it's the simplest way.' Health and Safety had not gone mad in those days.

When my parents decided to buy the car, Joan had not driven for years. During her youth in Paris in the 1950s she had kept a Triumph Mayflower, which she mainly used for weekend jaunts. One Saturday she and her friend Peggy were bowling down a country road in Normandy, gaining on a cycling farmer. When they drew level, Joan wound down her window to ask him the way, but she pulled in too close, causing the man to topple and fall off. On the same outing they failed to give a wide enough berth to a lorry, and it plunged into a ditch, shedding six layers of hay. Those were honest errors, but on another occasion the girls deliberately caused mayhem by sticking newspaper to the lower half of the windscreen; this obscured the steering wheel and, thereby, the fact that the Mayflower was right-hand drive. As they whizzed round the Place de l'Etoile in the rush hour, Joan driving and Peggy in the front passenger seat, the other motorists assumed that Peggy was the driver. When, at the agreed moment, Peggy shut her eyes and flung her arms into the air, they took her for a lunatic, swerved to avoid hitting the Mayflower, and narrowly missed a collision with each other.

Joan was miffed to learn that, before she could start driving again in England, she needed to pass another test. The preparatory lessons that she took from the British School of Motoring she thought were beneath her, but she was wise to have professional instruction, for it avoids the tensions of lessons from a friend or relation. My friend Abe, a small and fiery man, told me that the first lesson he took from his father, who is smaller and fierier, ended in a shouting match, and that in the second they came to blows. 'Not literally?' I said. 'Literally,' he replied. Joan's instructor advised her to suppress her Gallic exuberance, and in particular the constant use of the horn. She managed to contain herself during the test, but thereafter resumed hooting in the Parisian manner. The test, which she passed, took place in Purley, dismissed by her as a 'beastly *banlieu*'. Perhaps because she was raised in a working-class street in Birkenhead, her snobbery was especially acute when it came to places. A few years later, when we bought a country cottage in West Suffolk, she was dismayed to find that the postal district was in Essex. 'We're *really* in *Suffolk*,' she was at pains to point out to bored hearers. In fact, letters would get there whether or not Essex was mentioned on the envelope, for the wizards of the Sorting Office can infer an address from the sketchiest information. The full address of our house was Frogs Cottage, Goose End, Halstead, Essex CO9 4AK, and the phone number was Ridgewell 302. I received a Christmas card addressed to Oliver Black, Fog End, Fridgewell. A wizard had appended a caustic comment in crayon. Wizardry was practised also by the local vicar there, who was a member of the Magic Circle. He tore around the lanes in a green Ford Popular, with a sign saying 'YOU NEED CHRIST' in the back window.

The car we bought was a half-timbered Mini Traveller: 379 GLY. I can remember the registration plates of all our cars in my childhood – its successors were JLL 74D, SLD 20F, EGP 599J and MHX 836L – but now can't bring to mind the number of my current one. I choose to believe that this is due not to senility but to the facts, first, that in those days my memory had less in stock to compete with the plates and, second, that nowadays I concern myself with higher things. Mnemonics, if I stooped to them, would solve the problem: for GLY I had 'ugly'; for JLL, 'Jill'; for SLD, 'shillings, pounds and pence'; for EGP, 'egg pan'; and for MHX, 'mohawx'.

The Mini was an Issigonis original, that being the only model there was in 1964. It was later that the debased Clubman came on the market, and later still that the Mini was revived as a formless blob tricked out with a couple of eroded motifs from the original design. It's a depressing trend, the same having happened to the Fiat Cinquecento among others. Our Mini was brand new – it would not have occurred to Misha, who was fonder of spending than of getting, to buy a secondhand one – and the colour we had picked from the catalogue was Smoke Grey. In fact the car was pale blue, so, if the catalogue was not at fault, either we or Spuffords, the dealer, had got into a muddle. Spuffords' showroom (long since a Nando's) had in its window, apart from a couple of cars, a coach of the horse-drawn kind – a marketing blunder in the Swinging Sixties. The salesman, Mr

Sellers, was a juvenile drip, but in my eyes a high priest. On our test drive of the new car, he took the controls before handing them over to Joan, and I was struck by the contrast between the honeyed smoothness of his gear changes and the juddering lurches of hers. She continued to find the car a trial to drive: the gear lever was stiff, and the feeble cheeping of the horn failed to frighten other road users. She endured the frozen shoulder that the gears caused her, but replaced the horn with a blaring two-tone one made for long-distance lorries. That had the effect she desired. It was so loud that it made you jump when you were inside the car. As she blew it every few seconds, you were trembling by the end of a short journey.

I was delighted with the Mini, and especially with its new smell, but that was soon masked by stale Gitanes, for Misha would not only smoke in the car but insist that the windows be kept shut. It was often hard to see out. I wonder how much healthier and cleverer I would have been if my parents had not constantly exposed me to toxins. Misha's first act on waking was to light a Gitane, and he would then wander naked around the flat, the yellow cigarette hanging from his lip and shedding ash on his chest, where it caught in the hairs and threatened to shrivel or ignite them. Sometimes he smoked a pipe. As a baby I used to like sucking on his unattended pipes, and so Joan bought me a little one of my own. I didn't smoke it, of course, but was often seen being wheeled up and down the Strand in my pram, looking like a small Popeye with the thing sticking out of my toothless gob. One day, having tired of it, I hurled it into the gutter, it broke, I wailed, and so Joan bought me another. The process was repeated every couple of weeks.

Joan too liked to smoke, and both my parents enjoyed a drink. By the standards of the time they were not crapulous, but by modern standards it was a crapulous time. They were content for me to be a passive smoker, but, passive drinking being harder, they used to entice me with Arak Punch, some sickly sludge called Cherry Heering, and other intoxicating beverages likely to appeal to the very young. No doubt the idea, which I refuted some years later, was that, if you are brought up to treat alcohol as an incident of civilised life, you will not go on binges in adulthood. I can't remember a time when my parents were not plying me with the stuff; in fact, I was pickled for much of the time *in utero*, Joan being a lover of strong Dry Martinis, which raced down the umbilical cord and coursed deliciously through my tiny veins.

If you know about registration plates, you can tell from those listed above that we changed our car often. My parents were convinced that you got the most for it if you sold it within two years. After two years our Mini had clocked up 628 miles: Joan had collected me from school in it, she had driven us to the park on the odd Sunday afternoon, and we had once substituted it for the bus when visiting Moomps and Poops. (Joan offered to take Poops for a spin, but he declined with a shudder, having a Saudi opinion of women drivers.) That was about it, but my parents stood by their dogma and sold the car, for a tiny sum, to the son of a friend. The young man asked whether they had tampered with the milometer.

We packed more miles into our two years with the next car – another Mini Traveller – for by now we had Frogs Cottage, sixty-five miles from London. I hated the journeys there and back, for my nausea was aggravated by Misha's Gitanes. If I threatened to vomit, he offered me his seat in the front, but it never occurred to any of us that he should either stop smoking or open a window. On the return journeys I was distracted by *Pick of the Pops* with Alan Freeman, which my parents seemed to enjoy as much as I did. A car radio was a novelty. Joan found the gears of the new Mini as stiff as those of the previous one – she would have had a more comfortable time if we had kept either car long enough for them to loosen up – and now there was the problem of dipping the headlights. This had not arisen before, as the old car, not having gone further than Finsbury Park, had never had its light on full beam. The lights were dipped by pressing a remote pedal which Joan, whose legs were short, could barely reach. By the time she had pressed it, she had blinded the oncoming driver who had flashed angrily, blinding her in turn.

Then there was the anti-burglar switch, devised and fitted by our local garagiste: it was hidden in one of the side pockets, and when you pushed it forward the engine cut out. One winter Sunday night, when we were driving home from Frogs Cottage, Joan braked sharply, causing the big atlas that we kept in the pocket to slide forward and push the switch. The engine duly shut down. She could not restart it, for none of us thought of the switch, and so we sat there, in rural Essex, while the rain hammered on the roof and Rolf Harris sang 'Two Little Boys' on the radio. I remembered the switch two hours later, just as the AA man was drawing up. Car security was rudimentary then, and was little better two decades later, when Joan locked herself out of the Ford Escort she then owned. The Ford mechanic who rescued her explained how to let herself in if it happened again: 'Dead simple. Slide a loop of plastic tape through the edge of the window, hook it round the lock button, and pull the button up. Bingo!' You'd think a company representative would be cagier.

The mileage of the second Mini was boosted also by a trip to the South of France. We didn't drive all the way: the first leg of the journey was to Lydd airport, whence an antique plane carried both the car and us to Geneva. The plane held four cars, which entered through a door in its nose, and for the flight you sat in an unpressurised cabin at the back. The boiled sweet which the elderly steward gave you to stop your ears popping failed to work for Joan, who was deaf on touchdown. Once we were in France, and one of her ears was working again, she perked up, happy on her old territory. She would beam graciously at the crowd of villagers who gathered round the Mini whenever we stopped at a café.

Becoming a hunchback from the gear changes, she demanded that our third Mini Traveller have automatic transmission, but this caused trouble of another kind. When she was trying to park in a tight place, Misha got out of the car to guide her, but, not being a driver, he was a bungling giver of directions, standing in a place where she could not see his gestures. When she was finally in, she vented her annoyance by giving a big rev on the accelerator before turning off the engine. The car, still in gear, shot backwards and slammed into the one behind, breaking its headlight. Misha, who had only just stepped clear, almost had his legs broken between the bumpers. I loved the new gearbox: there was a clutchless manual override, and when I was sitting beside Joan she let me change gear. While doing so I would pretend that I was the co-pilot of a bomber. Moving the real gear lever was more fun than turning the toy steering wheel which, when I was very small, a family friend had attached to her dashboard to entertain me on the day we moved house. While my parents supervised the removal men, this kind lady drove me and my dual controls back and forth through the tunnels under the Thames. We finished up at a fair on Blackheath, where I won a goldfish.

Minis were all very well, but they were ridiculous beside the cars of some of my classmates at Chegley House, a genteel prep school in South Kensington. An American boy called Randy Zinn, the son of a diplomat, was driven to school in a Buick Estate, which his parents must have shipped from the US. You could have fitted a Mini in the back, which had an extra row of folding seats for an extended family or a large circle of friends.[1] Then there was Rupert Laughton, a pompous boy who came out with remarks such as 'You are incurring my displeasure.' He invited me for an outing to Box Hill in his father's vintage Rolls, which he called 'the Royce'. The prospect was exciting, but the reality hideous, for even before we had cleared London I was feeling sicker than I ever had in the Mini, and Laughton's drone was more stifling than Misha's smoke.

I gained cred on days when Misha hired a chauffeur-driven limo and dropped me off at school. Usually the car company sent a Humber – respectable enough, but neither a Buick nor a Royce – but when the Humbers were all taken we were given a big Daimler, of the kind used for funerals. The inside was lined in fawn-coloured suede and, like Zinn's Buick, it had extra folding seats. Usually, however, Misha would deliver me in a taxi. 'Pelham Crescent, and then we're going on,' he'd announce to the driver, who would sometimes fail to register the 'going on' bit, take another booking on the way to Pelham Crescent, and turf Misha out with me in front of the school. The bookings often came down a radio from a zombie in a control room who would intone 'SW7. SW7. Anyone for SW7? SW7,' and so on. These days taxi drivers receive bookings silently by computer, but you still get the mantras in mini cabs. When I was a child it didn't bother me, but Misha

---

[1] Zinn briefly wore a dental brace which, instead of fitting in his mouth, was attached by wires to the back of his collar; he looked like a monster from *Doctor Who*, and got so much flak from his schoolmates that he discarded the thing after a week, settling for crooked teeth.

would lean forward to shut the glass panel between driver and passengers – as he did, without a word, if the driver started to chat to him. This high-handedness embarrassed me, but we never heard the driver protest. Drivers also seemed not to mind Misha's addressing them as 'Cabby', which made me similarly uncomfortable. My father had firm views about taxis. One was that it is more comfortable to sit on the left, just as (so he asserted) you should avoid sitting over the wheels of a railway carriage. Another was that taxi drivers never have accidents. While he was voicing it to Joan, who was alarmed by the speed of the cab we were all in, we veered into the path of a bus which hit us on the right side, shattering the window beside Misha. The incident supported the first view, however – pursuant to which, and out of chivalry, he had offered the left-hand seat to my mother.

When I was a toddler, a car was any vehicle – I would point at lorries, buses and trains and cry 'Cah!' – but by the time I was at Chegley House I was a connoisseur of makes and models, alive to the nuances of status they reflected. Having since lapsed wilfully into ignorance and indifference, I despise those adults, usually men, who display the zeal I had as a boy. A dinner at a restaurant in Holland Park was recently blighted for me by an oaf at the next table who was trying to impress his date with a list of the classic cars he owned. Having reached the end, he brayed 'I just LA-A-A-ARV CARS!' He leant back smugly and tried to put his arm around her, while she pasted on a receptionist's smile. Once, when I was a lawyer in the City, I was hanging around in a room with my colleagues and some bankers, waiting for a meeting to start. To pass the time, they swapped boasts about their real cars, as Laughton and I had done about our toy ones: a Maserati was trumped by a Lamborghini, and the latter by a vintage E-type, which was trumped by a DB5. Seeing me gazing out of the window, one of the bankers called over to ask what car I had. I thought of saying a 1935 Lagonda, but feared that they would corner me with questions. The best reply would have been that I didn't own a car, but I foolishly went for the truth and said that I drove a Leyland Metro (a cast-off from my mother). The room fell silent. That evening, when I took the Metro to pick up my new girlfriend for supper, I left it parked next to a large Jaguar while I went to ring her doorbell. When she came down, I led her for a joke towards the Jag, and was dismayed by her peevish expression when I explained that mine was the car behind. It was a short affair.

If a classic car is beyond your reach, you might be gratified by a personalised registration plate; I often pass a house outside which are parked two cars, one with the plate '2 BE' and the other 'NOT 2B'.[2] Below that in the hierarchy are fins and spoilers, a row of extra brake lights across the rear window, and a dark green strip across the top of the windscreen. A couple of decades ago the strip often bore the names of the driver (STEVE) and the passenger

---

[2] At the door of a block near me, Shakespeare is the name next to the bell for Flat 2B.

(SHARON), but those have gone the way of woolly dice and nodding dogs. Then you are down to jokey stickers, also seldom seen now. My favourite was 'Flash your lights if you think I'm sexy!! I said just your lights!!!!'

Of course, my contempt for the car as status symbol is itself another form of snobbery. Not yet burdened by it at the age of thirteen, I persuaded my parents to run mad when replacing the third Mini. We have reached the 1970s, era of the famous Ford Capri. There was an earlier Capri in the sixties, a sort of racing Anglia, but no one remembers those, and none was as striking as the ordinary Anglia that we often saw in Chigwell as we drove home from Suffolk: it was covered in purple felt. The 'iconic' Capri of the seventies was quite cheap and had the engine of a family saloon, but it was dressed up as a sports car, and you could add accessories of the kind described above, such as mock ventilators, rally wheels, bucket seats at the back, and a matt black bonnet. The one I nagged my father into buying had all these trimmings. You might think that a designer would fear being seen in such a thing, but perhaps he expected people to take it as an ironic statement. In my eyes the Capri eclipsed Zinn's lumbering Buick and Laughton's nauseating Royce, and Joan too wallowed in its vulgarity. In the family album there is a photo of her proudly washing it in the drive of Frogs Cottage: she's wearing a lime green sleeveless top with matching flared trousers, all in towelling. She remained stuffy, however, about the pronunciation of 'Capri', which she insisted was 'CApri', not 'kerPREE'.

The Capri was followed by an ochre-yellow fastback Opel Manta, hardly less garish. During its incumbency, Misha died. Money now being tighter, Joan kept the car for longer than its predecessors and then replaced it with a series of secondhand runabouts, descending through the circles of ignominy from Escorts, via Fiestas, to the Metro previously mentioned. As she got old, she shrank to the point at which the sun visor no longer shielded her eyes. Floppy hats were a clumsy substitute, so a former colleague of Misha's at the Royal College of Art detailed a student to design a bespoke visor: when it was down, an extra panel slid out, leaving a bare few inches of windscreen through which Joan could peer undazzled. Her legs shrank as well, so that she needed to move the seat further and further forward in order to reach the pedals, but we never got to the point of asking the student to rustle up some extendable ones. Platform soles would have been an alternative.

Joan's capacity for alcohol decreased with her size. When we were staying at Frogs Cottage, we were invited to dinner by Toby and Jill Hebblethwaite, a couple who lived a few miles away. The Hebblethwaites being hearty drinkers, Joan and I agreed in advance that one of us would join in and the other stay sober enough to drive the Metro home. The toss of a coin condemned Joan to sobriety. 'Just the one, then, as I'm driving,' she said to Toby when, on our arrival, he offered her a G and T. Toby then poured an eighth of a bottle of Tanqueray Export into a glass, added a thimbleful of tonic, and handed it to her. Once it was down her throat, our agreement blurred in her mind, and I was too merry to keep an eye on her. By the time we reeled into the dining room, we had each had three such aperitifs. Over the main course, while Toby burbled on, Joan fell asleep, her head resting beside her plate. The rest of us decided not to notice, but, when Jill had cleared the plates and was setting out the bowls for pudding, I gave Joan a prod. She snorted, mumbled 'Wozzat?' and 'I wozznsleep,' sat up abruptly, gazed into her empty bowl, and then was sick into it. The vomit smelt of gin. She was so productive that Jill whipped the bowl away and shoved hers, and then mine, in front of Joan, who, once the flow had stopped, and after a few dry heaves, began to cry. 'Think nothing of it, darling,' Jill drawled. 'Toby's friends do far worse.' Since, of course, I had to drive home, I went very slowly – keeping below thirty on the main road, which was almost empty of traffic. A police car came up behind, pulled out and drew level with us, the rozzer in the passenger seat eyeing me suspiciously. I smiled airily. You can't win: they are after you if you go quickly or slowly.

In London, Joan mainly travelled by bus, to get the most out of her old person's pass. One day she got on the wrong one. As it was crossing Vauxhall Bridge, she went up to the driver and said 'Are you meant to be going over this bridge? You normally go over Westminster.' That shook his confidence, for he was new to the route. After a many-point turn, he struck off on an uncharted course, to howls from the other passengers.   Soon they were in darkest Lambeth, and the driver called out to ask whether anyone on the bus knew the way back, as pilots sometimes ask whether there is a doctor on the plane. A man came down from the upper deck and took charge.

Spotty and Horny

My friend Hamish had a stroboscope, at which he
would stare, claiming that this induced serenity.
When I was suffering from lethargy, he offered me a
go, but I declined, from fear of a fit. Perhaps, he
suggested, my problem was Seasonal Adjustment
Disorder, in which case a SAD light might do the
trick. This I was willing to try, so I bought one at
Peter Jones and stuck it under my computer screen,
whence it cast its kindly rays on me while I worked.
It was hard to see the screen, and my energy level and
mood were unchanged. Other therapeutic
illuminations I have tried were an infrared lamp for a
strained Achilles tendon – again no benefit – and, at
the opposite end of the electromagnetic spectrum, an
ultraviolet sun lamp for acne. The NHS provides
ultraviolet treatment for a number of skin conditions:
an acquaintance with giraffish patches goes once a
week to hospital where he stands in an ultraviolet
'shower', with nothing on except a black sock over his

genitals. I would have thought a white one was safer, as it would reflect more rays.

My treatment was simpler: you put the sun lamp on a table, pointed it at your face, and sat there for ten minutes, as fully clothed as you wished. The tan it gave me was implausible in two respects: first, it appeared in November – the father of a schoolfriend asked where I had found snow to ski on at that time of year – and, second, it was a lurid orange, unlike the tan you get from the real sun. So anxious was I to get rid of my spots that I overdid the sessions, adding peeling skin and the risk of melanoma to my original complaint. The lamp was one prong of a multi-pronged attack: I also had antibiotics; a cream called Neo-Medrone, which added a whiteish crusty veneer to my skin; and a soap called Acne Aid, embarrassing to request at the chemist. None of them did much good.

You will have gathered that I was a bad case. Many teenagers have spots, but mine were so many and so large that they merged into a mountain range, distorting the outline of my face. They looked their most hideous when reflected in the kettle, perhaps because the curve of the metal made them loom forward, so I would make tea with my eyes averted, shooting the odd horrified glance. My plight was made worse by the fact that I was at boarding school, with no relief from the comments of my classmates. One or two gleefully feigned sympathy, but most took the medieval approach, delighting in reminding me that I had become an object of revulsion. The chief persecutor was Jackson minor, who had gallingly sprouted bristles when and where I had sprouted spots. 'Aaaaaaaagh!' he cried when he noticed the flecks of blood that covered my pillow, and the other members of the dormitory gathered to stare, make similar noises, and then dance round me by way of exorcism. Once, on the rugby field, I and some others had to swap shirts, for the sake of uniform team colours; Jackson refused to wear mine, on the ground that I had pulled the collar over my rotting face.

My parents were small comfort. When they came to visit one weekend, my father put his arm round me and said 'Cheer up – I had awful acne too when I was your age,' adding, with something near a cackle, 'but not as awful as yours!' When there was a slight improvement, and my mother kindly lied 'You can hardly see it any more,' he chipped in 'No – so long as you stand with your back to the light.'

Despairing of the treatments listed above, I tried the scorched-earth method of applying neat Dettol. It made me smell like a public lavatory, but had no useful effect. To dull the misery, I would drink alcohol, but that brought blood to the surface, causing the rash to glow and throb. I also comforted myself by eating Heinz Sandwich Spread – the stuff that looks like sick in a jar – till I found that it too aggravated the spots; perhaps I should have applied it to my skin. I became friends with a boy called Perdue, whom I had shunned because he was so dim (his nickname was Gamma, for that was the mark he always got), but his obverse virtue was blindness to the state of my skin. Late one evening, when only he and I were in the washroom, and I was squeezing a gigantic boil in the middle of my forehead (Jackson and others had for the nonce christened me The Unicorn), a Niagara of pus ran down my nose and into my eyes while Perdue burbled obliviously on about his train set.

Of course I was not the only acne sufferer at my school, but I was the second-worst case. First prize went to a boy called Todd, who looked like the Elephant Man and took up long-distance running. When we met at a reunion, both of us middle-aged and smooth-skinned, I reminisced jokingly about our sufferings. Todd looked irritated and impatient. 'I don't know what you're talking about,' he said; 'I never had acne.' Odd how schoolmates turn out decades later. At the same reunion was Peter Passmore, a genial and self-assured man with a baby on his arm. At school he had been a timid child, known as The Drip, because he sometimes wet the bed. To encourage him to do so, we would wait for him to fall asleep, and then we would dangle his finger in a mug of tepid water. It was hard to tell whether this worked – as it was to know who won our masturbation races, conducted with torches shining on our knobs under the sheets, to cast phallic shadows. The self-proclaimed winner was always a camp specimen called van Pelt, who would shuffle off to the lavatory, fumbling with Kleenexes. We never demanded verification.

These competitions were as fleeting as greyhound races, so easily aroused were we at that age. During 'assignment' periods, when we were meant to work on our own, I would nip out, often three or four times a day, for self-administered hand relief. Leaning against the counter of the tuck shop, when queuing for a bun at break, was enough to give me – and presumably the other boys in the queue – an erection. It was not explained by the looks of Mrs Tufnell, the Bingo-winged proprietress, whose only striking feature was that she changed the colour of her hair every week – a fact possibly connected to her being the singer in a Dixieland combo which played the local geriatric homes. Mr Tufnell, who likewise combined duties (he was the saxophonist), was so thick that in our argot 'Tufnell' was a synonym for 'moron'. For illegal smokes we would buy matches in the tuck shop. 'Do you have Swan Vestas?' I asked Tufnell. 'No, only chicken curry,' he replied.

While sitting the chemistry O-level, I came spontaneously – not because of anything stimulating in the question (it was not biology), but just from tension and hormones. I was embarrassed to throw my encrusted Y-fronts into the dormitory's communal laundry basket, which Matron sorted through, but I reflected that probably other pairs in the basket would be similarly crisp, and that Matron would have learnt to take such things in her stride. A similar ejaculation at home, during some maths revision, posed more of a problem. If I threw my pants in with the laundry, my mother would be confronted with my dried semen – a toe-curling thought. If I washed them, and she saw them hanging up to dry, she would ask questions. If I threw them away, she would find them in the wastepaper basket, with the same result. My solution was to hide them under a loose floorboard in the attic: our flat was at the top of a Victorian block. A few years later, after we had moved, I noticed that the roof of the block was being replaced. There were my pants, with my school name tag in the back, waiting to be unearthed by a workman. Would he try to contact me – perhaps with a threat of blackmail? The thought haunted me for some years.

The Menace

As a boy I longed to drive a car. Now, in late middle age, I have no interest in driving and usually let my wife be my chauffeur. It's like other things I craved when young: to own a watch, to click my fingers, to have elastic-sided shoes, and to make a popping sound with a finger in my mouth. I have achieved them all and am bored. A Buddhist would draw a moral.

For the most part, the nearest I came to driving when I was a child was to operate our motor mower, a Suffolk Punch. For me 'Suffolk Punch' is primarily the name of a mower, not of a horse – just as people now associate 'crane' with lifting machinery rather than with birds. You could not sit on the Punch, but I still imagined myself to be riding a Harley-Davidson as I trundled up and down. It was in my parents' interest to encourage me: 'You do such lovely stripes,' my mother Joan would exclaim. When she wanted the hedge cut, she would try 'You do such a lovely straight top,' but that was less effective, having no fantasy to reinforce it.

When I reached sixteen, the year before driving-licence age, she sent me for some off-road lessons at Crystal Palace, where I bumbled around a track in an Escort, supervised by a toothless man called Mr Tune. The highlight was an afternoon's practice in skidding: an area surrounded by bales of hay was covered in oil, and you had to slalom through some traffic cones. Mr Tune told me to 'turn into the skid', a phrase that I didn't understand then and that still baffles me. When I reached seventeen, some on-road lessons enabled me to pass the test, although the examiner, a gloomy man in a bottle-green suit, nearly failed me for driving too quickly on side streets. Years later, when my friend Mike, who was working freelance as a driving instructor, kitted himself out to look smart for his pupils, he bought a suit of the same shade. Perhaps there were guidelines from the Department of Transport.[1]

The reckless streak noticed by the examiner broadened once I had my licence. My first victims were Joan and her old uncle Jack, whom I took for a spin in the family Opel along the narrow lanes near our weekend cottage. Not content with the prestige of driving, I reached for the lighter to start a cheroot that I had nicked from my father's box. While my eye was off the road, the car drifted to the other side and mounted the steep bank. Jack, in the back, shouted 'Ah, pah, ah, pah, pah'; Joan, next to me,

---

[1] Later renamed the Department *for* Transport, doubtless at a high cost in fees to PR consultants.

screamed, grabbed the wheel, and brought us down just before we would have tipped over. In the recriminations that followed, she alleged that the shock would kill Jack. If she was right, the effect was delayed by six years.

My mother took a dim view of drivers who didn't look where they were going. Whenever she was driven by her friend Peggy, who would turn to chat to her as they sped along, she would stare hard at the road ahead, in order to set an example and to alert Peggy to dangers. I recently came round to her opinion when I visited my friend Abe at his holiday house in the suburbs of Nice. One day he drove me into the hills behind the town, to show me the view. Although the road was steep, narrow and winding, he not only kept turning his head to look out of the side window, but would take both hands from the wheel – one to point, the other to gesticulate. While doing so, he would let his foot slide from the accelerator, and the car would drift to a halt. Sometimes we started to roll backwards.

Despite having experienced my recklessness, Joan allowed me to drive the Opel – quite a zippy car – without supervision. During a university vacation, when my friend Dan visited for an evening's hard drinking, I offered to drive him home to Dollis Hill. As we hit sixty-five on Ladbroke Grove, a blue flashing light appeared in the mirror, but I failed to notice it until we had stopped at a traffic signal. Getting out of the car, I lost my balance and rolled on to the road. 'You don't care if you lose your licence or not, do you, chummy?' the policeman said to me with standard irony, his face hardening when I prattishly replied 'Not really – I'm at Cambridge most of the time and have little use for a car.' After I had blown the breathalyser bright red, he ordered me into his car, his colleague taking charge of the Opel and Dan, and we drove in convoy to Willesden police station. The result of the breathalyser now had to be verified with a sample of either urine or blood. As I was dehydrated by alcohol, I plumped for blood, but I was bursting with pee two hours later when the doctor arrived with his syringe. Drunker than I, he jabbed several parts of my arm before finding a vein, and when he had taken the sample he upset the bottle, spilling the blood over the floor. I dare say I could have refused to shed any more, but I meekly sat there while he jabbed me again.

There was a court hearing, to which Joan insisted on accompanying me. Having arrived early, we sat through the trials of various petty crims before it was my turn. When we entered, a barrister was saying 'My client would like 120 similar offences to be taken into account.' We cast glances at the fiend in the dock, a crestfallen young man in an ill-fitting suit, who turned out to be a fare-dodger. Next up were three boys who had set fire to a railway carriage; their counsel had a cock-and-bull story that they had started the fire in order to dry their wet clothes. When I was called, I walked to the front of the court, where there was a bar at groin height, presumably for you to hold on to if you felt shaky. Puzzled by its position, I leant forward and rested my elbows on it, so that I was lolling in front of the magistrate. It probably didn't help my case. I was banned for a year, given a fine of £200 and, when I asked for time to pay, told that I should have saved up in the months since I was charged. Joan called from the back of the courtroom that she would settle the bill. A mortifying morning.

During the year of the ban, I relied on friends for transport. My girlfriend abided by the principle that one should not weave between lanes, and so, when she drove me up the M1 in her ancient Riley – we were going for a weekend of passion in Ballachulish – she tootled along at sixty in the fast lane, ignoring the flashes and hoots behind. Even that modest speed required her to keep her foot hard down, with the result that after a few hours the accelerator's spring lost its springiness and the engine would run only at maximum RPM. She didn't notice until we left the motorway and found ourselves tearing along unclassified roads.

Wild joyriding resumed as soon as I got my licence back. One night during the Cambridge term, I crashed a friend's Renault; the friend himself was unable to drive, having fallen asleep in his own vomit after coming third in a 'How many Pernods can you drink?' competition. I was not injured, although I deserved to have been turned into a vegetable. (What kind would I have been? Broccoli, perhaps.)

It's appalling to think that there are drivers at large who are as I used to be. Since those days I have largely kept clear of the law, otherwise than by being a solicitor, and now consider myself a staid motorist, although there was one occasion, decades later, when I again nearly lost my licence for alcoholic driving. Having drunk more pints than I should have, during an evening out with Mike, I was driving back to my flat in the Barbican. I was going steadily enough but, in my dreamy state, had forgotten that the City was surrounded by the Ring of Steel against the IRA. At the checkpoint the policeman motioned that I should wind down my window and bent down to ask me where I was going to. 'The Bah-ah-ah-bican,' I replied, engulfing him in beery fumes, some directly from me, others having built up in the car on the way. Again the breathalyser went red, again I was driven to the nearest station to have its results confirmed. 'Do you want a solicitor?' asked the policewoman who took me there. 'I am a solizzer,' I replied. Pee and blood had now been replaced by a machine into which you blew. The woman told me to purse my lips around the nozzle and blow hard. Having grown cannier than I had been when I let the drunken doctor take a second sample of blood, I gave a feeble puff, letting my lips flap. She told me that, since according to the machine I was just below the limit, I was free to go – her tone and smile making it clear that she had seen I was cheating. Perhaps she found the stern talking-to that she gave me more gratifying than the rigmarole of making a charge.

Had the policewoman challenged my blowing, I might have replied that alcohol is known to play havoc with the embouchure – a fact I had confirmed, at first and second hand, as third trombonist in the military band at my public school. Once we went to play at a nearby school for girls, where we were treated to tea, including unlimited cider, before the concert. The performance was a shambles, and the journey back in the coach a near riot. When the coach stalled going up a steep hill, the sousaphonist, a small boy called Charles Darwin, who was sitting near the front, vomited his cider and cake into the aisle, down which they then advanced, to the roars of his fellow bandsmen.

As that case indicates, brass players have a weakness for strong drink – a paradox, given the point about the embouchure. A friend of mine in a German orchestra tells me that their third trombonist – my counterpart – was such a drunkard and glutton that one evening, when they were all eating at a restaurant while on tour, he threw up over the table, then covered the product with an upturned bowl and carried on eating. Thereafter he would dine alone, the other musicians refusing to sit with him. His career ended when he fell through the stage and broke his back. There was a whip-round, but it failed to collect much. I wonder if his driving was better than mine.

Road Hogs of the World

For most of the time before I married Fluffy, I didn't own a car. When I was writing my PhD thesis, I used to take a bus from London to my mother's weekend cottage in Suffolk, where I would stay in the hope that the peace of the countryside would aid concentration. As anyone knows who has made the comparison, the country is noisier than the city. In spring the local farmer planted rape, from which he would scare the birds with a gas-powered device that exploded every two minutes. I would sit at my desk, girding myself for the next bang – just as, in the university library, I would wait for the next click of the clocks, the hands of which moved forward synchronically every thirty seconds. I noticed the clocks only because I hid away in the library's quietest part, the Slavonic Bibles section. If you are neurotic about noises, you will find one to disturb you wherever you are, even if it is only the surging of blood in your ears. As I type, a chaffinch is repeating *itchiwitchaweeweeCHWEEOO.*

Among the regular passengers on the bus, which started from St Pancras and stopped at the bottom of our lane (among other places), was a woman who gabbled to herself. Once, when I was in a seat by a window, she sat next to me and kept it up all the way to Harlow. I was too nervous to climb over her knees and find another place. When I could avoid such distractions, I tried to use the time for reading, but this sometimes made me sick and sometimes drowsy. Drowsiness can be a harbinger of nausea: I am told that, if you rock a baby for long enough, it will throw up if it doesn't doze off. The M11, up which the bus used to go, may have a *virtus dormitiva*: a friend used to get his small son to sleep at night by driving him up that motorway as far as Stansted. The paediatrician warned that the child might come to take this sufficient condition of sleep for a necessary one. You never know what will work: another friend lulls her baby by playing on the iPhone a recording of a hairdryer. She also has one of a vacuum cleaner, which is just as effective.

If I fell asleep on the bus, I would be able, when I woke up, to read without feeling sick. In that roundabout way, I got through a lot of Proust, himself a soporific. As the bus reached our lane at about eight-fifteen in the evening, I could, if I got my skates on,[1] walk up the road, let myself in, turn on the heating, prepare a crude supper, and be in front of the

---

[1] My friend Dan says that this phrase originates in the sexual practices of Atlantic fishermen. Apparently the genitalia of the female skate resemble those of the human female.

telly by nine o'clock, just in time for *Minder*, my favourite programme at the time. I was delighted when my mother told me that it was on again. 'New series?' I asked. 'Of course I'm serious,' she replied, her hearing then on the wane.

The only car I owned before my marriage was a black Mini which had belonged to our neighbour in Suffolk. She went gaga shortly after buying it, and it sat unused in the shed during her dotage. When she died I bought it from the estate at a knockdown price, congratulating myself, for it had fewer than 1,000 miles on the clock. The congratulations were misplaced, for a blue tit had nested under the bonnet, mice had eaten through the tubes, and rust had detached the exhaust pipe. When I did get it on the road, I had several near-misses, other drivers failing to notice a small black vehicle. I should have fitted a frightening horn, as my mother had on her own Mini years before.

During my time with the car, I verified a claim that I heard on a radio programme called (I think) *The Locker Room*, a male equivalent of *Woman's Hour*. It was that men let themselves weep in circumstances where there are sure to be no witnesses; a nocturnal drive on a motorway was said to be a favourite. Only a few nights previously, while I had been driving alone up the M11, it had occurred to me how dreadful it would be when my mother died, and I surprised myself by bursting into tears. It may have been an offence under the Road Traffic Act. When she did die, I was relieved, for she, like our neighbour, had been miserably senile beforehand.

Once my mother was no longer able to drive, I took over her Leyland Metro, which I kept, at great expense, in the car park underneath my flat in the Barbican. The car park was manned throughout the day and night: the attendant would sit in a hut, reading the paper, eating his supper, smoking, watching porn films on a portable telly, or snoring, depending on the hour. The car-park men would take deliveries for you to collect from the hut; I had my clean laundry left there till I noticed that the shirts smelt of stew and Golden Virginia.[2] As the space was expensive and I had little use for the Metro, I put the car up for sale on the intranet of the law firm that employed me. There was a surprising variety of things on offer there, including a rabbit: 'Needs a firm hand,' the caption said. The lawyers ignored my advertisement. There was only one expression of interest, from a secretary, who, having inspected the car, declared that it would be bad for her image.

Most of my driving was in hired cars. One spring I used one to take my friend Rebecca round the Peloponnese. I was nervous about this, for the Greeks have the reputation of being the worst drivers in Europe – or is it the second-worst? They are rivalled, I think, by the Portuguese. I have no bad memories of the other road users, but I do have them of the roads, which changed unpredictably: one minute you were bowling along a broad highway, then you rounded a corner, the road abruptly ended,

---

[2] The laundry service itself was unsatisfactory, my shirts shrinking by two per cent every time they came back. It mounts up.

and you found yourself bumping along in a field. You also never knew what obstacles were in wait. When we skidded to a halt inches from a large lump, we found it to be a tortoise on its back, its scaly legs waving. I got out and righted it, and then let it make its own way to the roadside, a process that took some time. Rebecca became impatient, but I was keen to minimise contact with the animal, after a similar experience with a mole near my mother's cottage. The poor blind creature had been shuffling along the road, so I picked it up in order to place it in the grass. When I did, it seized me with its claws, causing me to drop it. After several similar incidents in Greece, I grasped that I had to keep my eyes fixed to the road surface, and I was therefore unable to enjoy the views that Rebecca kept ecstatically pointing out. It was even more annoying when we reached the Mani and she started singing 'We're in the Mani' to the tune from *42nd Street*. If I annoyed her, she would cry 'You're driving me round the Peloponnese.'

I have little evidence to judge Portuguese drivers, but they must be better than Brazilian ones. I am told that the people of Brazil look down on their former colonial masters, and my impression is that Brazilians generally are proud of their nationality. The one who delivers takeaways for our local Chinese always announces, as soon as you open the front door, 'I am from Brazil!' (which he pronounces 'Brazeeoo'). I don't much care, but I smile politely. He is also pleased with his name, Heinrich O'Flynn – an instance of the onomastic promiscuity that prevails in that country. When it comes to driving, the

Brazilians have nothing to boast about. I discovered this on holiday in Rio, where I stayed with a lawyer called Ramona, who lived just behind Copocabana beach, in a flat that stank of jackfruit, with two servants and a poodle called Rico. Ramona would always shout the dog's name, giving a long prefatory gargle to the R, thus: Gr-ch-gr-ch-gREECO! I did not discover the names of the servants, one of whom was mute and the other, during my visit, had a psychotic episode. Because the mad one had to be taken to hospital, dusk was falling when we set out in the car for Ramona's fazenda, sixty miles out of town. To make up time, Ramona put her foot down. If she came up behind a slower-moving vehicle, she did not decelerate, but held her hand on the horn while she overtook – on the inside if need be, even if we had to plough along a soft verge or mount a pedestrian walkway. Her brio, matched by other drivers, was striking in a woman who must have been in her late fifties. When I asked Ramona how old she was, she tentatively replied 'Fifty?' as if it were an opening bid for negotiation.

More frightening still than the Brazilians are the Indians. I have twice been on driving holidays in the subcontinent – once in the 1990s, once in the 2000s, both times in an Ambassador, which, although new, had a design from the fifties; you got up, rather than down, into it. On the first trip, my girlfriend and I were driven around Rajasthan by one Pandy. His English was scant, but he knew to say 'Lench?' at lunchtime and, whenever we passed a camel, would say 'CamEL'. As the animals are common in

Rajasthan, it became tiresome. If we asked him something, or gave instructions, he would wobble his head in the Indian way – something between a nod and a shake, which seems to mean 'I have heard and am going to ignore you.' Although a gentle person, Pandy drove maniacally, as did his compatriots. It was standard practice at night to drive without lights, and at all times to play chicken, aiming at the oncoming vehicle until, at the last second, one or other of you swerved. I tried to believe that, since all Indians drove in that way, they would have adapted and learnt to avoid accidents, but the corpses at the roadside thwarted my attempt. The only way to stay calm was to fix my eyes on things inside the car. That made me queasy, and undermined the purpose of the trip.

Indian drivers are more considerate of animals than of each other. At a roundabout – or 'rounding', as Pandy called them – on the main road into Delhi from the airport, a skeletal cow had lain down, perhaps to die, on the carriageway, causing a queue. It being sacred, no one tried to move it, or even hooted at it. There were also a couple of donkeys, just as thin, ambling among the stationary vehicles. As we sat there, I had time to study some roadside advertisements, for Seventh Up, Thums Up, and something called Earthquack, which was claimed to be Top Natch. Mellow Bra and Panty was another one.

On the second trip, I and three friends were driven around Tamil Nadu by Mohan, a man of military mien. Every night, having dropped us at our hotel, he would bed down in the car. As we set off in the morning, we would cautiously sniff for stale farts and cast our eyes around for stray socks, but the car was always fresh and spotless. Mohan had a sovereign method of asking for directions: pulling up beside a male passer-by, he would wind down the window, continue to stare ahead through the windscreen, and twice shout the name of the place we were making for. Thus, when one of our party wanted to visit a sandlewood factory, he barked 'Sandlewood Sandlewood!' It was surprising how often this worked.

My friends were keen on Chola temples. Each of these was magnificent, but after I had seen a few they merged in my mind. Whenever we turned up at one, we encountered the same group of excitable young men dressed in black; they were Dikshitars, Mohan told us. He would drive us to the gate, we would leave with him our shoes – forbidden in the temple – and our valuables, and then we would wander through the vast complex of buildings. At one place I lost my friends and my way to the exit, and I feared that I might be stranded there, shoeless and walletless. It would be no good asking for help, for I could not remember the name of our hotel or even of the town it was in. An old, thin, white man with a long beard shuffled past me, possibly abandoned by his friends and driver years before and wandering the precincts ever since.

A Crook Mitre

Twelve years ago, when I had bronchitis, I went to Vera, my GP, who listened to my chest and back. She was uninterested in my bronchi, but picked up an odd sound from my heart. 'I'm sure it's nothing,' she said, 'but I'll send you to a cardiologist. Thomas McPhee is very good.' I broke into a sweat, for I knew that in Vera's mouth 'I'm sure it's nothing' meant 'I'm very worried'. If it meant what it said, why was she sending me to a cardiologist?

When, a couple of mornings later, I arrived for the consultation, the receptionist told me that McPhee was still in the theatre and that in the meantime I was to have an echo in the basement. I was baffled. Who put on plays in the morning? Was I to shout in the cellar, and did the volume of the echo show something about my heart? 'Echo' turned out to be short for 'echocardiogram', a process that produces ultrasound images of the heart: electrodes are stuck to your chest, you lie on your side, and the technician runs a microphone, lubricated with gel, over your torso and neck. In the basement I was greeted by Wendy, an alarmingly young thing, who, after I had removed my shirt, tried to attach the electrodes with a kind of gaffer tape. They kept falling off, and Wendy's hands started to shake. 'I do know what I'm doing,' she said, confirming my belief that she didn't.

She was rescued by a Scottish woman with a Morningside accent and a hockey-sticks manner, who introduced herself as Jean. This was the technician, and Wendy, I was relieved to be told, was a trainee. 'Ooooh,' Jean exclaimed as she slid the mike around, 'this is much more fun than a normal heart! Look,' she said to Wendy: 'even you must be able to see what's wrong here.' In a whisper, I asked what she had found. 'Floppy mitral valve – very floppy indeed,' she said with glee, and showed me a moving image of two flaps which were meant to shut snugly at each beat but which swung feebly and erratically as if in a breeze. 'You'll have a prize-winning murmur with that,' Jean went on, and, turning a knob, filled the room with a squelching and hissing sound that came from me. I was appalled by the squelching, but it was the hissing that I should worry about, she told me, as it was the sound of blood leaking back through the valve.

Having managed to wipe a small portion of the gel from my chest, I was sent upstairs to McPhee, now back from the theatre, for the official diagnosis. A large and loud man with a clubhouse-bar manner, he waved me to a seat while he glanced at the images that Jean had sent to his screen. 'Yes, well, well, squire – no need to panic,' he boomed, and, seeing me start to panic, added 'Ha ha – that is, no need to worry, ha ha ha!' The phatic reassurance over, he gave me his standard lecture on prolapse of the mitral valve, and the regurgitation of blood that it causes. I was a 'moderate' case, but my condition could worsen as I got older, in which case the valve might need to be repaired or replaced. 'But you'll probably be fine, dear boy,' he went on; 'it's more likely that something else will kill you first – ha ha ha ha!'

I asked about the operation. 'Pretty straightforward,' said McPhee, 'and techniques are improving all the time. Now they're starting to do it by remote control with keyhole surgery. It's all done on a screen: your surgeon could be sitting in the hospital canteen, having a cuppa and a Mr Kipling.' Not finding the image a soothing one, I asked about the old-fashioned method. 'Open heart,' McPhee replied, making his chair crack as he leant back and rested a brogued foot on the mahogany desk. 'First they open up your chest' – in my mind's eye a chainsaw squealed through my breastbone, dispersing a cloud of dust, and two nurses opened my ribcage as if it were a pair of barred gates – 'and then they take your heart out, stop it, and pop it in a box to work on. They keep you going on a heart-lung machine. When they've finished, they pop your heart back in again.'

I hate the jolly-you-along use of the word 'pop'. At a recent check-up, the nurse said 'Will you pop your pants down for me?' in the way that air hostesses

like to say 'Will you pop your seat belt on for me?'
'For me' is in the same category. I asked McPhee
how they got the heart started once they had popped
it back in. He put the other foot up on the desk and
started to chuckle. 'One colleague of mine gets his
team to stand round the table and they all shout "Go,
heart, go!"' The chuckle blossomed into another
braying laugh. 'It's a very safe operation: only a one-
in-fifty chance of something going wrong.' Those
odds sounded quite high to my ear. What did he
mean by going wrong? 'Kidney failure, stroke, or
death. HA HA HA HA HA!' His shoulders heaved
like Ted Heath's, and his chair cracked so loudly that
I expected it to collapse under him.

He put his arm round my shoulder as he saw me
to the door, and told me to come back once a year.
Each time I did so, I was struck by the contrast
between Jean's dire animadversions – 'Ach, yes, it's
flapping like a pair o' wee sails: you'll need a new one
soon, no doubt about that' – and McPhee's back-
slapping cheeriness: 'You're fit as the proverbial, old
chum. Very naughty of Jean to treat you to her *obiter
dicta. Experto crede!*' He seemed to have taken Latin
lessons since we first met.

More convinced by Jean than by McPhee, I asked
Vera to refer me to another consultant, so she sent me
to Mark Fale, a man at the funereal end of the jollity
spectrum. He scowled when he greeted me, and
during the echo, which he carried out himself, he
shook his head, sucked his teeth and sighed. He
dismissed me to the waiting room while he examined
the images, and then, having summoned me into his

consulting room, offered me a chair in the manner of one about to break terrible news. His opinion coincided with Jean's: the prolapse was severe, as was the regurgitation, and an operation in the near future was almost certain. Given the state of the valve, a repair was out of the question: I would need a mechanical valve, which would itself wear out in a few years, and I would have to take Warfarin for the rest of my days. I was too shaky to ask how many days those would be. He would, he said, see me every four months, to ensure that my heart, already distended, did not expand to a dangerous size – in which case an operation would be too late.

At each of these sessions, on listening through his stethoscope, Fale would announce that my murmur had got louder. How could he tell, given that the listenings were months apart and that he heard hundreds of other murmurs in between? No doubt he was softening me up for the operation. 'Are you *still* feeling all right?' he would ask. I thought so, but, when a doctor asks you that question in that tone, you hunt for symptoms. These, he told me, would be tiredness, breathlessness and palpitations. Thereafter I felt constantly bushed and so short of breath that I could barely climb the stairs, and I would walk around with my hand pressed to my side, registering every skipped beat. He once had me fitted with a twenty-four-hour monitor of my heartbeats and blood pressure. Every hour a ring would inflate around my upper arm. At night this of course woke me up, usually in the middle of a gothic dream which I would otherwise have forgotten. It brought home to me how much more interesting it is to be asleep than to be awake.

Fale himself looked ill. Although quite a young man, he was overweight and pasty, and his breath smelt of old cabbage. For some months our front hall had a similar smell, which we traced to a dead rat under the floorboards. When I phoned to make an appointment for my fourth check-up, his secretary said 'Unfortunately, Dr Fale has died.' 'Unfortunately', which came from the same stable of mealy-mouthedness as 'pop' and 'for me', was the wrong word in my view, for I hated the man. 'Oh dear, how dreadful – I *am* sorry,' I replied. 'May I ask what he died of?' 'A myocardial infarction,' said the secretary, at home with the jargon, and explained: 'A massive heart attack.' Heart attacks, when mentioned, are always massive.

I was right to treat Fale's death as a stroke of good fortune, for I was passed on to Professor Hart, the first cardiologist I have both liked and trusted – in fact, the first I have either liked or trusted. Having assured me that my condition was stable and needed to be reviewed only once a year, he declared that my murmur was so crisp that it would be a shame not to let a student hear it. Would I mind? I consented, and he summoned a spotty girl called Trixie, whom he invited to listen to my chest. Applying the stethoscope, Trixie settled into a gormless expression. As she seemed to be getting nowhere, and the proximity of her acne was making me uncomfortable, I threw out a clue: 'Not a bad murmur, eh?' Hart whispered to me not to give the game away, but he too became impatient, and dragged an opinion out of her by Socratic questions, in answering which she confused systole and diastole. I hoped that, if such people ever qualified, they were diverted to minor organs.

I used to think that, if I had something serious wrong with me, I would want to know. Now I am less sure. If Vera had not noticed the murmur, I would not have had all those examinations, which were prudent of course. But I would still be standing here today, and have been spared twelve years of anxiety.

Freedom Pass

One of the miseries of old age is the keeping up of appearances that no longer match reality. You need to look smart, but your bunions are killing you, so either you hobble around in leather shoes or your carpet slippers contradict your suit and tie. You are trying to follow a conversation, but your hearing aid is on the blink, so you nod and smile at what you hope are the right moments. The way to avoid these vexations is to give up the fight, for the young are mostly willing not to hold their seniors to the standards they require of themselves – and, if they aren't, they are too flinty-hearted to be worth impressing. In particular, the old enjoy an especially broad freedom of expression. I plan to take full advantage of such tolerance when my time comes, and to welter in florid, offensive senility. Some say that I have started early.

The struggle of the old to seem young can be an unsettling spectacle. At a recent lunch party I was squashed against an antique flapper, who twittered, giggled and pouted, her coy moues cracking her impastoed make-up, thick enough for a pantomime dame. Her front teeth were false, but she still had the odd real molar, to judge by the putrid smell that puffed out of her when she laughed. This was partly masked by a sickly odour hard to place – somewhere between Chanel No. 5 and Harpic – which increased in strength when she shifted her bottom. As I was meant to be eating, nay enjoying myself, I tried not to draw connections with my aged neighbour Dicky, who had come round the day before to collect a couple of large boxes labelled 'TENA Incontinence', which the postman had left with me. I had been going to drop them off, but Dicky must have needed them urgently. 'Gosh, I wonder what these are!' he chirruped as I handed them over. 'I wonder!' I replied, just as brightly.

No, far more dignified to make the best of being frankly old. My friend Sue keeps her mother Connie in a flat on the ground floor of her house. Twenty years ago Connie had an eightieth-birthday tea party, and Sue invited some of her own friends – thirty- and forty-somethings – for moral support. We mingled for a while with the oldies and then drifted upstairs, where the talk stuck on mortgages, nannies and local schools. It was clear, from the increasing racket beneath, that Connie and her chums were having a much jollier time: one of them was bashing out wartime favourites on the piano, others were warbling along, and the rest were shouting over the singers. Having a rented flat, no children, and thus nothing to add to the conversation on the first floor, I went down again and ruminated with Connie on the favourite subjects of the different cohorts: my lot droned on about mortgages, in your fifties it was pension plans, in your sixties you boasted that, even though you had retired, you had never been busier. What did Connie and her friends like to talk about? 'We compare rest homes,' she replied.

Last week it was her 100th-birthday party, and she had few friends left to invite. Those who were there no doubt compared undertakers. Sue again invited some of her own age group, this time to bulk up the numbers. Connie and I sat next to each other on the sofa and chatted, as we had twenty years before; she was still alert and sparkling, although physically frail. I was awestruck in the presence of one so old; it occurred to me that the date of her birth was nearer the age of the stagecoach than to the present day. She introduced me to a couple called Reeny and Norm: Reeny had been a schoolfriend in the early 1920s and had been married to Norm seventy-five years. They were hard work. If you looked Norm in the eye and addressed him, he would reply with animation; but, as soon as you stopped stimulating him, he would slump like an abandoned string-puppet and gaze at nothing. Reeny kept asking him whether she had been to the lavatory.

A person who makes the most of old age's freedom of expression is Mrs Fenn: she was introduced to me as such, and I don't know her first name. The introducer was my friend Lettice, an Oxford don, whose daughter was being christened in the college chapel; Mrs Fenn and I were both invited to the ceremony, and Lettice asked me to accompany Mrs F there on the train from London. The latter is in her eighties and shouts what might be called old-fashioned opinions in a *Brief Encounter* accent. In the Paddington ticket office, where we joined a snaking queue of silent martyrs, a Sikh man with beard and turban was on duty. 'Very warlike people, the Sikhs!' boomed Mrs F. The silence of the other queuers grew thicker. In my mind's eye this Sikh rushed from behind the counter, whipped a curved dagger from his Network Rail jacket and sliced off Mrs F's head and then mine. In reality, either he was atypically pacific or he had not heard, but to be on the safe side I suggested to Mrs F that she might be more comfortable waiting on a seat outside while I bought the tickets. Off she wobbled in her high heels. When I emerged I found her on a bench, next to a West Indian man who was reading a paper. 'Don't know why we kowtow to the racial minorities,' she called to me as I approached. 'What about the racial majority?' It was hard to tell whether this was a random outburst or referred to her neighbour, who, looking uneasy, moved off to another seat.

Our platform was at the far end of the station, and on the way there Mrs F kept stopping, to volunteer further observations; she seemed to find utterance easier when she was not moving her legs. 'What a frightful scrum,' she said, gesturing at the crowd with a sweep of her umbrella. 'Who *are* all these people? Where do they think they're going? Why don't they *stay at home*?' I suggested that their reasons for travel might be as weighty as ours, but she shouted over me: 'I tell you what would clear a bit of space: someone should *plant a bloody bomb* on the concourse!' A large man in a leather jacket stepped in front of us and produced a card. 'I'm a police officer,' he said to me. 'We don't find that sort of comment amusing, sir. It causes alarm and despondency. I'd suggest that you say nothing further, or I'll have to place you under arrest.' I apologised in a servile way. It would have been useless to point out that he had been addressing the wrong person: if you accompany a wayward oldie, other people take you to be responsible for her/him. It's the same with dogs.

Our progress was so slow that we missed our train. By the time we reached the chapel, the baby had been done and the service was almost over; but Mrs F clattered up the aisle to sit near the front, I felt obliged to stick beside her, and so I was glared at by the rest of the congregation, who applied the principle of responsibility just mentioned. The noise we created drowned the quavering mumble of the chaplain – another old person, but with a miserable fraction of Mrs F's vim. At the reception that followed, I hoped to give Mrs F the slip, but she made it clear that I was to be her walker for the day. The vim fortified by three glasses of champagne, she turned the volume up to max and treated me to her views of the other guests. We were standing behind a woman who was wearing yellow stockings, like Malvolio's, only not cross-gartered. 'God Almighty!' cried Mrs F. 'What on earth has that woman got on her legs? She looks like a seagull in stilletos.' The seagull must have heard, but decided not to respond.

Mrs Fenn's rudeness was largely explained by high spirits. My mother Joan, in old age, was ruder still, but in her case the cause was mental decay. Joan in her prime had been sharp-tongued, and, as senility set in, the tongue became sharper. I took my friend Hamish to visit her. The last time they had met was twenty years before, when Hamish had been slim. Now he was fat. 'Eugh, you're fat!' were Joan's opening words. 'Yes,' Hamish replied ruefully, 'I don't know what to do about it.' 'Take exercise. Eat less,' was Joan's reply, after which we could not get another word from her.

The dementia advancing, sharpness of tongue developed into outright aggression. When Joan was too far gone to look after herself, she was visited twice daily by Oyebola, from Social Services. This lady lacked the polish of the Faubourg Saint Germain, but was kindly enough, and seemed to rub along with my mother, but one day, as I approached the flat, I heard shrieks through the front door. I found Joan, in her pee-soaked petticoat, brandishing a mop, chasing Oyebola round the bedroom, and alliterating fortissimo 'You beastly bloody black bitch!' Social Services sent me a letter stating that they would not tolerate racial abuse, and again I had to grovel vicariously: the attack was due to dementia; my mother, when she had possessed her marbles, would not have dreamt of abusing other races; some of her best friends were black – so ran my letter in reply, most of it untrue.

When Oyebola went on holiday, Joan spent some time in a local hospital where old people who would otherwise have lacked care were dumped. She was in a long Victorian ward with a row of beds down each side; the first time I visited, I didn't recognise her in the parade of scarecrows propped against the iron bedsteads. Around a table in the middle of the ward, four bored nursing assistants – all foreign, all very young – sat leafing through magazines and neglecting their helpless charges. One old girl was trying to drink a cup of tea, but her hand shook so much that the scalding liquid was pouring down her front. 'Oh dear, oh dear,' she was cawing to herself, as the outline of her withered breasts became visible under her soaking nightie. A junior doctor had just finished dressing a sore on the occupant of the bed next to Joan, and I asked him whether he knew anything about my mother's case. He was brusquely dismissive, as if I had been a beggar. Joan justifiably took a dim view of the place, and expressed it in forthright language, of the kind she had used during the mop incident. Her neighbour, whom the doctor had been attending, was stuffy and genteel – perhaps the widow of a judge or a general – and took just as dim a view of Joan's choice of vocabulary. 'Honestly!' she exclaimed. 'Do we *have* to listen to this? Disgraceful!' She glared at me (of course), I smiled apologetically back, and I murmured to Joan that she was disturbing other patients. My mother turned to the stuffy lady and shouted 'Fuck off!' The latter picked up a newspaper and rustled it impotently.

Low inhibition, exhibited by my mother and Mrs Fenn, shades into low self-awareness, also common among the old. In particular, they are often unconscious of the noises they emit. In the cinema, watching a romcom, I was next to an old man who kept up a commentary to himself: 'Ah ha, oh gosh, look at them, good heavens, what a surprise, well really, she's a bit of a goer.' After ten minutes of this, I turned and hissed 'Will you please be quiet. I'm trying to enjoy the film too.' He looked at me briefly and blankly, then turned back to the screen and resumed the commentary.

My mother's uncle Jack, who would motor down (as he put it) from Birkenhead to visit us when I was a child, was similar. He liked to be kept busy, so my parents would prepare a list of odd jobs, which he always finished on the first day; thereafter he sat around, drumming his fingers on the arm of the chair. While doing the jobs he would sing to himself. Over the years, he had garbled the words of his favourite songs, so that, for example:

Where'er you tread
The blushing flowers shall rise

came out as:

Where'er you fled
The flushing powers shall rise.

He tended to muffle the words, perhaps in imitation

of the seventy-eights on which he had first heard them. Thus:

Sweetest little fellow, everybody knows

became:

Swmmtmmst lmmtlmm fmmllmm
Mmvrmmbmmdmm knmm.

When he was bored with singing, he would whistle through his teeth. On one occasion the job he was thus accompanying was the mending of the doorbell. The medley of ding-dongs and Swmmtmmst lmmtlmm fmmllmms became too much for my mother, who finally begged him to be quiet. Jack was taken aback, for he had no doubt thought that the song was going on in his head, and you can't mend a bell without ringing it.

As well as favourite songs, he had favourite sayings, one of them, apropos of drivers, being 'It's not what you do, it's what the other fool does.' His driving was based on folk maxims of this sort, for he was old enough never to have taken a test. When I was small, he had one of those bull-nosed Rovers, the horn of which he allowed me to press twice when we set off anywhere. 'Two toots and we're oot!' he would cry as I did so. Later he had an Austin 1100 and reclined the driving seat so far that, from the outside, he appeared to be a midget sitting in the back. He was safe enough driving along the middle of country roads at thirty miles an hour, but was out of his depth in London, where he was constantly harrumphing at what 'the other fool' was doing. He enjoyed such wordplay, once tricking me, when I was little, with a matchbox in which, he said, there was a green bee. I slowly pushed the box open. It was empty, but on the bottom Jack had written a large B in green. Then there was the visit to the park to see the 'rose-coloured swan', which of course was white.

Jack was a vigorous man – he would march around swinging his arms, like one of the Red Army on parade – but long before his death my mother became convinced that he would not be with us much longer, and so she gave him increasingly lavish presents on his birthdays. Lavishness being measured, in her eyes, by durability, Jack left behind an assortment of radios, Teasmades and electric shavers in fine working order.

Similar to Jack in the songs and sayings department is Ron, a friend's father-in-law, whom I caught whistling the old jingle 'If you like a lot of chocolate on your biscuit, join our CLUB.' When I remarked on it, he was as startled as my neighbour in the cinema and as Jack in the case of the doorbell. Ron's sayings are less witty than Jack's were, and are always preceded by 'I always say'; he could thus truly say 'I always say I always say'. What follows is usually beyond dispute – for example: 'I always say it's a good idea to bring a woolly once the evenings start drawing in.'

A more debatable case, as regards the degree of self-awareness, was Solly, late grandfather of my friend Dan. Solly, a Jewish refugee from Berlin, never learnt decent English and he refused to believe that his grandson knew German, despite Dan's often speaking to him in that tongue. Solly subsided into depression and hypochondria, and the only sentence he would utter to Dan was 'It's a terrible sing to be o-o-o-o-ld.' He would shuffle around the house in his dressing gown, quietly howling to himself, while his wife Friedl shouted 'Vy doesn't he *shut up!*' When Solly thought that there was no one else around, the howling would segue into the jaunty humming of cabaret songs from the Weimar era. He perked up generally after Friedl died.

As that case indicates, the trials of old age often cause self-pity and small-mindedness. Beth, mother of my friend Alan, was a cheerful and kind woman in her prime, but now her chief pleasures are to complain and to embarrass. In Kleinian terms, she has changed, in Alan's eyes, from the good breast to the bad breast, but he describes her as the bad Thora Hird, for she was born in Morecambe, has kept her accent, and facially resembles Thora. When Alan could no longer bear his mother's moaning about her ailments, he took her to the doctor, but on arriving at the surgery Beth assumed a brave and smiling face. 'I'm fit as a fiddle,' she said to the irritated GP, whose time was short. 'I can't think why my son has brought me here.' On the bus home, the moaning started again.

Its usual object is stomach ache – advanced, at the last minute, as a conclusive reason for not attending her own eighty-fifth-birthday party, which

Alan and his sister had taken weeks to arrange. Beth dropped this bombshell while her mouth was full of a Mr Kipling's Angel Slice, one of six that she consumed in rapid series. She is seldom far from a cake or biscuit, and likes to hold a column of shortbreads between thumb and middle finger as she potters around her bungalow. With that fact in mind, Alan and I took her for a treat to a teashop, but nothing there met her approval. 'This tea is a bit wet,' she said, wrinkling her nose, so Alan fetched her an Abbey Crunch to mop it up, but this was too hard for her teeth. 'Eating this biscuit is *agony*,' she declared, loud enough for heads to turn. With a sigh, Alan suggested a piece of chocolate cake. Beth assented, but when the cake was brought she pushed it away. 'I like chocolate,' she said, 'and I like cake, but I *dawn't* like chocolate cake.'

Despite her protests about the state of her tummy, Alan cajoled her into a brief appearance at the birthday party, but she was grumpy while there, sprinkling animadversions on others in earshot. 'Look at 'er,' she said of a niece just across the table. 'Talking about herself as usual. She hasn't got one redeeming feature.' Of the niece's husband, sitting right beside Beth, she said 'I can't think why you've sat me next to him. I've always hated him.' As in my mother's case, Beth's outspokenness is due in part to senility. When she was diagnosed with dementia, Alan phoned from her bungalow to give his sister the bad news. 'It's early-stage Alzheimers,' he murmured so that his mother, in the next room, would not hear. '*Very* early-stage!' Beth called out.

In rarer cases the suffering ennobles. Molly, nonagenarian aunt of my friend Mike, caught the rubber foot of her walking frame in the crazy paving, toppled on to her back and paralysed herself from the neck down. It was a dreadful coda to an active life – in her youth she had been a champion at show jumping, an activity more likely to cause paralysis – but Molly was serene as she lay in her hospital bed. 'Things could be worse,' she said to Mike when he visited, and he was tempted to ask how. Lacking stimulation, her mind started to wander, and she was certain that the village policeman was going to rescue her through the window. 'A donkey came to visit me yesterday,' she said one Christmas Eve when most of the other patients had been sent home for the festivities; 'he was wearing a hat.' 'How lovely,' Mike said, saddened by this fugue, but as he was leaving the ward he bumped into the sister, who said 'A local farmer brought a donkey in here yesterday to cheer up the patients. They loved it. The donkey was wearing a Santa hat.' On her better days, Molly would prattle away, only her lips visibly moving. When she started to make scurrilous comments about her neighbours and their visitors, Mike would drop a grape into her mouth. Samuel Beckett would have loved it.

Similarly serene, in circumstances similarly hostile, was Joseph Dampf, a pianist, also in his nineties, whom I heard accompany a Norwegian contralto in a concert of Scandinavian lieder at Wigmore Hall. Usually it is the audience, rather than the performers, at WH who are notable for their advanced age: if you want to feel young, a trip there is as refreshing as one to the Supreme Court or the House of Lords. Quite a few of the old folk go alone. When I entered the auditorium for the recital, I noticed my colleague John Horrocks, an ancient philosopher in both senses, sitting by himself in an aisle seat, reading the *Lesser Hippias* with a large magnifying glass. Walking past, I tapped him on the shoulder and greeted him. He jumped and let out a small shriek, causing the same reaction in the solitary old lady in front of him, who had been reading *The Tablet* unaided.

When Dampf and the contralto came on to the stage, they made an odd pair – he tiny and twinkly, she vast and scowling – and she had to hold him up as he shuffled to the piano stool. At the end of the first half, when Dampf stood to take a bow, his trousers fell to his ankles, revealing baggy yellowish boxers and spindly greyish calves. Despite the rhubarb of horror in the hall, he didn't realise what had happened, until the singer bent down and helped to pull the trousers up. In Dampf's position I would have fainted with mortification, but he smiled sadly at the audience and gently shook his head, as if to say 'It's a funny old world.' The applause was rapturous, though no one risked a standing ovation.

During the interval, I noticed the couple in front of me, on the first row, right by the stage. It was another ancient man – clearly gaga – and, judging by appearance, his son, who kept fussing over him and was just as clearly terrified that the old boy would say or do something embarrassing – although you might have thought that the recent sight of the pianist's pants would have persuaded anyone that Wigmore Hall was Liberty Hall. The lights went down again, and Dampf and the contralto reappeared, the trousers of the former now pulled up to the breast bone and secured with green string that contrasted with the white tie and tails. A few bars into our second dose of hyperborean gloom, the father in front of me started to cough loudly, attracting a frosty glance from the singer. The son whipped out a lozenge, which he then unwrapped very slowly; no doubt the intention was to minimise crackling, but crackling there was, and it lasted for nearly a minute, during which the coughing continued. Eventually they quietened down, and the performers moved on to the darkest number so far, about a suicidal lover in a pine forest. It was tailing off into *ppp*, the audience gripped and silent, when my old friend in front shouted 'WHERE'S MY PUDDING?' The contralto was so rattled that she strode off the stage, leaving Dampf, who was unable to walk without assistance, sitting at the piano, smiling and shaking his head as he had done over the trousers.

My interest in the SWOT matrix for old age is more than, as they say, academic, for the twilight years begin at sixty, and I am nearly fifty-nine. My wife Fluffy, imbued with the Young-As-You-Feel ideology, hotly denies that people in their sixties are old: for her, old age is thirty years more than her current age, and twenty more than mine. In that case, I shall never be old – which is sad for both of us, because she claims to like old people best.

I am resigned to being old, and am looking forward to some aspects of it – the Freedom Pass in particular, which will allow me, on idle days, to whizz up to Cockfosters on the Piccadilly Line for free; or I could go round the Circle Line a few times, as a friend used to do in order to acclimatise to London when on holiday from a Brazilian shit-hole in which he had found a job teaching philosophy of mathematics (there was none going elsewhere). It's a shame that trains on the Circle no longer go round and round, but follow a snail-shaped route that requires you to change at Edgware Road. Since, however, you only have to cross the platform, that should not be a problem for another decade or two.

Resigned to age I may be, but I am deluded about my appearance. I look at men of my own age and take them to belong to my father's generation, even though my father, if alive, would be 105. The most recent issue of the old boys' magazine from my school contained an article about a cricket match, one team in which comprised 'boys' from my year. My classmates of forty years ago, mainly unrecognisable, were fat, bald, wrinkly, and/or otherwise disgusting. The only exception, I thought, was James Crawley (known in our day as Creepy), who was shown with his family and seemed to have stood the test of time quite well – but then I realised that I was looking at his son, and that Creepy was the wizened relic next to him. It doesn't occur to me that I look like these people: in the shaving mirror I see the fresh, taut face of a man in his thirties. The delusion is stubborn, like that of the anorexic who looks in the glass and sees the Michelin Man. It's the same when I am asleep: in dreams I am twenty- or thirty-something, explicitly or implicitly, and the jump of two or three decades on waking is a shock.

I am forced to face reality when I visit the Three Minute Man – as my barber is known, because that is how long it takes him to cut your hair, unless you want something fancy, which his clients never do, it not being that sort of establishment. His trick is not to chat: there is nothing about football scores, or where you are going on holiday – just a brooding obmutescence. I welcome it, and would use my time in his chair to collect my thoughts if he did not have Kiss FM on so loud. Only once did I try to start a conversation: 'I came round last week, but you were shut. Have you been on holiday?' TMM: 'Burying me father.' OB: 'Good Lord, I *am* sorry.' TMM: silence.

When he has finished giving me a Number Six on top and a Number Three elsewhere, he holds a mirror behind my head, so that I can approve his craftsmanship at the back. It reveals the badger patch of grey, of which Fluffy makes fun and I deny the existence, and, in place of the dense thicket that my mind's eye sees, the scrubby wisps that spiral around my crown. While holding the mirror, the Three Minute Man bends down, so that his face is next to mine, and I can compare and contrast them in the mirror over the basin. He is fit, in his thirties, and his face looks as I imagine mine does. Mine is saggy and careworn, and looks like Creepy Crawley's.

When the Three Minute Man increased his prices, he told me that, because I was a client of long standing, he would continue to do me at the old rate. 'Still ten pounds to you,' he grunted under his breath, in case Kiss FM didn't prevent his other clients from overhearing. 'Very decent of you,' I murmured back, merrily adding 'It's like being an OAP.' 'Oh, sorry: OAP?' he replied. 'In that case it's nine pounds.' Given our low decibel level, I decided that it was too hard to unravel the misunderstanding, and since then have enjoyed the OAP rate. Thus encouraged, I now, when visiting a museum or gallery, always ask whether there is a reduced price for old people. No lie is involved, for the question is enough: without asking for proof, the infant behind the desk hands me a concessionary ticket. In this respect I *have* started early.

Permissions

'Shrunk': A shorter version was published in *The Lancet Psychiatry* 2015, volume 2, issue 2, pages 126-7. Reprinted with permission from Elsevier.

'London's Leading Hypochondriac': A shorter version was published, under the title 'Gadding About', in *The Lancet Psychiatry* 2016, volume 3, issue 1, pages 26-7. Reprinted with permission from Elsevier.

'I'd Love to Take Orders From You' (Dubin, Warren). Permission to reprint approved by Warner Chappell.